LATER
CHAPTERS

THE APPLAUSE ACTING SERIES

LATER CHAPTERS

THE BEST MONOLOGUES AND SCENES FOR ACTORS OVER FIFTY

COMPILED AND EDITED BY

DIANA AMSTERDAM

APPLAUSE
THEATRE & CINEMA BOOKS
AN IMPRINT OF HAL LEONARD LLC

Published in 2018 by Applause Theatre & Cinema Books
An Imprint of Hal Leonard LLC
7777 West Bluemound Road
Milwaukee, WI 53213

Trade Book Division Editorial Offices
33 Plymouth St., Montclair, NJ 07042

Printed in the United States of America

Book design by Lynn Bergesen, UB Communications

Library of Congress Cataloging-in-Publication Data

Names: Amsterdam, Diana editor.
Title: Later chapters : best monologues and scenes for actors over fifty /
  compiled and edited by Diana Amsterdam.
Description: Milwaukee : Applause Theatre & Cinema Books, 2018.
  | Includes bibliographical references and index.
Identifiers: LCCN 2017052717 | ISBN 9781495072475 (pbk. : alk. paper)
Subjects: LCSH: Monologues. | Acting—Auditions.
Classification: LCC PN2080 .L37 2018 | DDC 808.82/45—dc23
LC record available at https://lccn.loc.gov/2017052717

www.applausebooks.com

CONTENTS

Scenes

FOREWORD

by Diana Amsterdam

My first play was produced nearly forty years ago. As a very young playwright, I wrote about people my age—as I think playwrights tend to do. Now that I'm older, I am no longer interested in the coming-of-age stories of twentysomethings or the new parenting experiences of thirtysomethings.

The lives of people over fifty are infinitely more interesting. Life tempers and life teaches. Compromises and sacrifices, hard-won wisdom, sweet savoring and appreciation of pleasure, knowledge of true worth and value, greater confidence and self-acceptance: These are what make our "later chapters" truly fascinating. As Martha Patterson, one of the playwrights selected for this book, has a character say, "Nothing in life turns out just as you think it will."

But where are the plays for us? Although we comprise most of the theatergoing audience, there are precious few.

And where there are few plays, there will be few parts for actors over fifty. Most of the actors who performed in my first produced play, *Fast Girls*—from which I've excerpted a monologue for this book—are no longer acting. Four of the five characters in that play are in their twenties. Those actors have matured and gone on to other things.

The vast majority of those determined to "make it" as actors in their twenties have dropped out of the profession by their late thirties. Unable to make a decent living, and tired of the audition grind, they leave the profession while there's still time to build a career elsewhere.

So who does stay?

Actors over fifty are the most determined, committed, and passionate people I know. Most have had parts on TV and in movies but haven't been able to count on that income as a regular stipend. If they have been acting since their twenties, they are veterans; they are the seasoned ones, the dependable ones. They know their way around a reading; they can work successfully with the overinflated egos of temperamental directors; they arrive on time, and they know their lines. They get to the heart and core of a character as if by instinct. They are trained by acting classes, workshops, showcases, off-Broadway stints, and lifetimes of learning their craft.

I know actors, working actors, who would handily win Tonys and Oscars if their great talent were given that chance. But they remain in the realm just under stardom where they still must struggle to make a living and be recognized. Despite this, they stick with it. Acting is what they do; acting is their gift and they need to give it.

Then there are the folks who return to acting or begin an acting career when they are past fifty. They have a good chance of getting roles, especially if they are male. When auditions are called for older actors, the hallways don't *line with actors* as they do with the younger crowd.

This book is the anthology for all of you: dedicated lifelong actors, and new and returning ones. *Later Chapters* is a bonanza of never-before-compiled monologues and scenes handpicked *specifically for you.*

You can pick up this book and find an exciting audition piece or acting-class scene. Your talent is appreciated; there are playwrights writing *for you.* I hope you'll recommend the plays excerpted here to theater companies. Encourage the theater world to include you, and all of us—after all, we are the ones who buy tickets.

Finally, I decided to compile this book because I and my friends are remaking each age as we come to it. I hear a lot of that rubric, "Sixty is the new forty," and variations thereof. Actually, sixty is the new sixty. We don't do sixty like our parents did. We aren't sitting by the side of the road, or the living room, watching the young people flirt, create, produce, and influence the world. We are the influencers.

Most of the pieces in this book have been previously published. (There are a few exceptions.) This is because most publishers want to give the actor access to the complete work. I found this stipulation—that work be previously published—a bit limiting. I didn't want pieces about Alzheimer's (although there is a great one in this book) or about cute, doddering old inmates of nursing homes who kiss with their lips extended like shelves. I wanted work that reflects *who we are today:* dynamic, productive, sexy, confident, and constantly striving. Many of the previously published works that I read portray mature folk as caricature.

I worked hard to find pieces that are original, authentic to our reality, and representative of the diversity that makes America great.

Notes on Using this Book

All pieces take place in the present time, except when noted.
It is okay to cut down a monologue for your use.

The term "Circumstance" is used at the top of each piece to
present location and context. When the Circumstance is absent
or scant, you can usually deduce the context and location from
the text itself.

If you relate to a particular role but are not the exact age of
the character as noted, that should not be an impediment.

For more information on obtaining the complete text, refer
to "Play Sources and Acknowledgments" on p. 165.

Diana Amsterdam
July 2017
Diana@dianaamsterdam.com

ACKNOWLEDGMENTS

This is the first time I've compiled an anthology for Applause. I wish to thank Carol Flannery, editorial director at Hal Leonard Performing Arts Publishing, for her patience in helping me through many learning curves over the past six months.

I thank Emma Goldman-Sherman, the ever-helpful connector of people, for putting out the call for submissions throughout her vast networks. Thanks to Emma, I reconnected with some writer friends and made new connections with talented playwrights.

We'd still be stalled in details if it weren't for the editing help of the guardian of consistency, my text editor, Timothy Paulson. And I have to give sincere praise and thanks to Lauren D'Errico, the young intern at Theater Resources Unlimited who worked with me to gather permissions in writing from an array of publishers, agents, and playwrights.

Finally, when I wasn't sure if I'd gathered sufficient selections, Bethany Jacobson provided a scene from one of her screenplays, *Hotel Bleu*—a wonderful scene. While I didn't end up using that scene, I thank Bethany for her generosity.

MONOLOGUES

ABSTRACT NUDE

by Gwydion Suilebhan

CHARACTER: MARK, early fifties

CIRCUMSTANCE: Mark speaks to friends about his parenting style. The audience or group members may take the place of his onstage friends.

MARK: Oh, don't you dare look at me like that. You don't know the truth. None of you do. I am not a villain. Children need order. I give Edward rules. All she ever gives him is permission. She says yes to everything. Yes. It's the absolute worst thing a parent can say to a child. Yes, you can have more ice cream. Yes, you can flunk out of math if it's too hard. You can undermine your parents' authority, take advantage of other people, use them, treat them like objects. Go ahead, do whatever the hell you want. We support you. Yes. The whole world's like this now. Yes. You're like this. You're definitely like this. You're all like this. You're all just desperate to have somebody, anybody, stand up and be an adult and say No, that's not okay. No, you're not allowed. Stop. But do you have any idea how hard that is to do? What it costs? Don't you think I'd love, absolutely love, to allow things? To permit . . . everything? Or God forbid to have somebody say yes to me once in a while. Yes! I would! But if nobody hangs on to that rope . . . people get hurt.

ADORATION OF THE OLD WOMAN

by José Rivera

CHARACTER: BELEN, sixty+

PLACE: A one-bedroom concrete house in rural, near-future Puerto Rico

CIRCUMSTANCE: Speaking to a younger woman, Dona Belen reflects on the power of her youth.

BELEN: You could tell by my hips I would bear a hundred powerful children. I couldn't read but I knew everything there was to know about men and women. I had a sense of humor. I could sing. I could carry my own weight in barrels of water and bundles of sugarcane. I could slaughter pigs. I could love all night. And men are so stupid, they have the very best, yet they're never satisfied. They sniff the air. "Ah, I smell some available pussy over there." How much more pussy does a man need, I ask you! Toli had a Caribbean queen. But it wasn't enough for him. He wanted the Mulatta Whore of Las Arenas. It was my destiny to love a man other women adored. I could have picked an ugly man, a monkey who smelled like piss. No. My man smelled like honey. Well, nobody takes what's mine! I had sixteen brothers and sisters and if I wanted a drink of water or a cup of rice I fought them all like a savage and I got what was mine—even with hookworms eating my guts!

JAKE'S MONOLOGUE FROM

AN ARTFUL MARRIAGE

by Martha Patterson

CHARACTER: JAKE, middle-aged

CIRCUMSTANCE: Jake paces back and forth in a luxury high-rise apartment.

JAKE: I'm a businessman. Self-made. Did it on my own, after graduate school and getting married. Own five Armani suits. Don't wear any jewelry except a Rolex. . . . I had an affair once, with a twenty-something who came into the office one day. Cute, sharp, well-dressed. It lasted three months. The wife never found out about it. Thank God. I can't afford a divorce; she knows my worth and I'd never be willing to part with a dime. It ended because the girl wanted to get married and, well . . . I already am! Not my fault, is it? . . . Been married twenty years. It's just easier this way . . . staying together, no alimony. Look, I've seen men lose a fortune over a crabby ex-wife. Why should I put myself in that position? In *Fortune* magazine it says men who stay with their wives are worth more. (*Sighs and sits down on the sofa.*) I guess I'm a bum. I cheated on her. I keep wishing there was something more ahead for me. Something that would make me feel young again. Sex? Hardly ever have it with her. She gained weight, doesn't look the same as when we met. I do. Haven't changed a bit. Even my hair's not grey. (*Pauses.*) I don't know if she realizes it yet, but I'm staying with her. She kind of puts up with me. And that's a very good thing. . . . I have regrets. I guess that's the thing. I wish I'd been faithful. I wish I hadn't cheated on my wife. She never did on me. That's what I love about her. She's got faith. I married a good woman. It's all about knowing what you have.

ARTIFICE

by Anne Flanagan

CHARACTER: EMMA, a middle aged British PhD who has disguised herself as an urbane New York art critic

CIRCUMSTANCE: The man she has obsessed about all her grown life is dead. Still, at a private showing of his art, Emma accuses him of having jilted her, and of ruining her life.

EMMA: You never rang me! You never rang. You said you would. You said you had a lovely time and you would fancy seeing me again and, as you were leaving, you said three words. Three little words. Three words that many say but few mean—I'll. Call. You. I never heard from you again! I waited. For months. *Years.* I waited, thinking of nothing else, willing the phone to ring. But nothing, *nothing* for ages—and then, after eleven years, three months, and two days, I learned that you'd gotten married. Married! I was upset, naturally, but I thought, well, maybe he didn't—maybe it's just a rumor or maybe it's true, but a marriage in name only, one of convenience, or perhaps she tricked you and you had no choice. At any rate, I continued to wait, faithfully, for you to make good on your promise. When I read about your death, I had to know—what were your last words? Did you call out for me? I retraced your footsteps to that miserable little Tibetan monastery. It was hard to get the monks to talk, what with that vow of silence and all—and how do you threaten someone who regards death as a promotion? Finally, I found a weak link. A real blabbermouth. Brother Tsing! He told me that you were alive and headed back to *her* and I had to face the awful, unforgivable truth. You were not going to call me. Not then. Not ever. And because of your betrayal, because of your selfish duplicity, because of *this*, I can no longer trust. Not you. Not anyone! Thanks to you, I've not been able to maintain any meaningful relationships.

BOY SMALL

by MT Cozzola

CHARACTER: **NEIGHBOR**, a retired woman in her sixties

CIRCUMSTANCE: Neighbor watches the house across the street.

NEIGHBOR: Something over there ain't right. It's not my business. Maybe I shouldn't be calling. I'm nosy. My pop said it, now my daughter says it. She says, what you need is another dog. I said, why? When I die you gonna get another Ma? Henry wasn't a dog. He was Henry. I see the girl going back and forth. I used to see the boy. Lately I never see the boy. Maybe there wasn't a boy. Maybe he didn't live there. Do I have to give my name? And the man. Something not right about him. Used to be an A-hole, now he's all neighborly. Probably wonders what else I got to get rid of. My dog Henry was one hundred percent Bernese. My daughter kept saying Bur-MEEZ. I said Bur-NEEZ, Bur-NEEZ, oughta call him Bernie so you remember. But Henry's what we went with. Henry loved that crate. Every night, ten o'clock, he'd go stand by the door. He'd stand there and look at me and I'd go, Okay Henry, go to bed. And he'd go in there and curl up and go right to sleep. After he passed, I couldn't look at that damned crate. I gave them the whole thing for practically nothing. But that's not why. I mean, I was happy to do it. I don't want bad feelings. But he was the best listener, the way he'd look in your eyes. My daughter said yeah, he's listening for Bacon Henry, Cheese Henry. She told me not to call. None of your business, Ma. Get a dog, Ma, keep you out of trouble. But if I did, I don't even have a crate. I guess that's why I did it. Yeah. In honor of Henry. So I won't be tempted, you know? Yeah. I can hold.

BREEDERS

by Bob Ost

CHARACTER: **RITA**, somewhere in her sixties

CIRCUMSTANCE: Rita is a painter of large canvases of flowers. Careful in her speech, accurate in her observations. Always kind, but never indulgent. She speaks to Carl.

RITA: We hope for some things—we spend years imagining what they might be like . . . This isn't the way, Carl. I've dreamed of us together, but this isn't the way. . . . When I left you, and came home to marry Colin, it was an enormously difficult decision. I've always been rather bad at deception, and that may have been the first time I ever felt the deep need to deceive. I wanted Colin to believe I really loved him. But I was in love with you, you old fool. Oh, I did care for Colin, but he loved me so very much. Such imbalance. But I married him, had the baby, and for the next twelve years, I gave up painting, and devoted myself to running the house and raising my daughter. I gave up painting, though many times Colin offered to convert the garage into a studio, but no, I had convinced myself that I wouldn't have time to paint. Of course that was utter nonsense. I simply needed to punish myself for all that deception. I can no longer live with deception. You must stop ignoring the fact that I have a daughter. How odd to think about her after all these years, not quite real, like a warm, lovely painting I can't seem to forget. I'm haunted by details: skin, hair, eyes—and an expression on the face, one frozen expression: a look of disappointment. (*Pause.*) She's never forgiven me for being gay. And I have spent so many years here with you, watching you hate, resent, and punish people for being straight—breeders, as you call them. Well, Carl, I am also a breeder.

CLASS

by Charles Evered

CHARACTER: **ELLIOT**, middle age

CIRCUMSTANCE: In an acting studio in New York City. Elliot addresses the audience as though they were his acting students.

ELLIOT: Oh, look at you all. Warms the cockles, doesn't it? A new fresh-faced batch of acting students. Positively bright-eyed and bushy-tailed. Ironic though, because even though you possessed enough of something to make it into this class, the truth is: most of you will never make it. The overwhelming majority of you will never make a living as an actor, the harsh reality being: you will probably spend thousands of dollars you don't actually have, in pursuit of a dream that will remain elusive. You will take out loans, you will borrow from friends, sleep on couches into your thirties and forties—your adolescence will be extended until it's embarrassing to everyone around you; holidays will become hell for you, as you sit around the family dinner table and your parents quiz your more successful siblings, only to eventually settle upon you—and after an interminably awkward pause, you will regale them with stories of the unpaid Equity showcase you just appeared in, in which you earned subway fare and free bagels—and were directed by a creepy trust fund idiot who made you dress up like a carrot-shaped dwarf. Yes, welcome to your future, ladies and gentlemen. The upside? Well, if things work out, you can perhaps change the world— or at least your little corner of it. You will know the sublime sensation of practicing an art that is more than honorable— and before you die, you may very well touch the hearts of tens, hundreds, thousands, who knows—maybe even millions of people you never met before, and in doing so, perhaps change their lives as well. But, as I've mentioned—that probably won't be happening to anyone in this room. Just so we're clear. Now, let's get started, shall we?

DEATH AND THE MAIDEN

by Ariel Dorfman

CHARACTER: ROBERTO, around fifty

CIRCUMSTANCE: A country that is probably Chile but could be any country that has given itself a democratic government just after a long period of dictatorship. A beach house by the sea. In the darkness, we hear Roberto's voice.

ROBERTO: I would put on the music because it helped me in my role, the role of good guy, as they call it, I would put on Schubert because it was a way of gaining the prisoners' trust. But I also knew it was a way of alleviating their suffering. You've got to believe it was a way of alleviating the prisoners' suffering. Not only the music, but everything else I did. That's how they approached me, at first. The prisoners were dying on them, they told me, they needed someone to help care for them, someone they could trust. I've got a brother, who was a member of the secret services. You can pay the communists back for what they did to Dad, he told me one night—my father had a heart attack the day the peasants took over his land at Las Toltecas. The stroke paralyzed him—he lost his capacity for speech, asking when I would avenge him. But that's not why I accepted. The real real truth, it was for humanitarian reasons.

We're at war, I thought, they want to kill me and my folk, they want to install a totalitarian dictatorship, but even so, they still have the right to some form of health care. It was slowly, almost without realizing how, that I became involved in more delicate operations, they let me sit in on sessions where my role was to determine if the prisoners could take that much torture, that much electric current. At first I told myself that it was a way of saving people's lives, and I did, because many times I told them—without it being true, simply to help the person who was being tortured—I ordered them to stop or the prisoner would die, but afterwards I began to—bit by bit, the virtue I was feeling turned into excitement—the mask of virtue fell off it and it, the excitement, it hid, it hid, it hid from me what I was doing, the swamp of what—. By the time Paulina Salas was brought in it was already too late. Too late.

FAST GIRLS

by Diana Amsterdam

CHARACTER: MITZI, fifties or sixties

CIRCUMSTANCE: From a New York brownstone, Mitzi calls her helpless doctor husband who is by himself, taking care of himself in their Florida home.

MITZI: (*Dials phone, into phone.*) Henry? Hello, Henry, how are you? T-t-t-t-t-. T-t-t-t-t-. T-t-t. T-t. I'm still in New York. No. No, she won't. I don't know, Henry, I'm trying. I called Max's. They're delivering. Rare. Baked. Cake. I left you four teacups with the tea bags, all you have to do is add the water. Yes, boiled, of course, the sugar is in the cupboard. The cupboard? The cupboard is next to the sink. The sink. In the kitchen. The white room. Look now. (*Beat.*) You can't find it? It says, "Sugar." It's yellow, Henry. The sugar is in a yellow box marked sugar, behind the red salt. Try. (*Beat.*) Can you believe the man can heal hairline fractures with lasers but he can't find the fucking sugar? Hello? You what? You cut yourself? How did you manage to cut yourself on a sugar box? On the salt. Wash it out. Go wash it out, Henry for God's sake, you're a doctor, wash it, put—a Band-Aid. In the medicine cabinet. In the bathroom. The other white room. I'll get home as soon as I can. (*Hangs up.*) Men!

IRONING LIFE

by Mary M. McCullough

CHARACTER: VIOLA SMART, a young sixty-year-old mother

CIRCUMSTANCE: Viola enters dragging a laundry basket with a large purse on top of laundry in basket. Takes head scarf out of purse, ties it around her hair. Viola tests iron with wet finger. Takes nail file out of purse, sits, talks to daughter, offstage.

VIOLA: Are you still crying in there? Is there something you're not telling me? I spent the first five years of my marriage crying. Crying if your father criticized me for anything. I'd cry if he said that I had burned the pork chops, back then when we ate pork. I tried cooking them like he said his Mama did, fried brown in the iron skillet with some grease. Cooked past the last roundup. In those early years, I was inexperienced in everything except that Cinderella love story. I wanted him to say, *"Oh, honey, these pork chops are so delicious. I am the luckiest man in the world to have such a good cook for a wife and a beautiful one at that."* Then I could say, *"Thank you darling but I did burn them a tiny little bit."* I mean I could admit to him that they were burned beyond recognition if he didn't notice. But he had to let me KNOW he NOTICED, sounding all critical, yelling about my cooking. I'd start boo-hoo-ing, telling him how if he REALLY loved me, he wouldn't act the way he was acting. You know what I do now. If the food is burned, I just serve the damn burned meat to him anyway. Once he told me, all polite like, "If you're using some different kind of seasonings, you don't have to serve this to me again." See. I made you laugh. Your father and me laughed a lot. I do love a man who knows how to laugh. Does that man of yours know how to laugh? Because a good laugh will take you over those marriage bumps, open the way for you to go on from where you are. (*Gets up. Tests iron again.*) This iron ain't getting hot. (*Checks cord, finds it unplugged.*) Honey, why don't I take these shirts to the laundry, get them ironed, and pick us up some Chinese.

WHAT REMAINS

by Martha Patterson

CHARACTER: **JEAN**, sixty-two, a widow, proud, practical, and genteel

CIRCUMSTANCE: A porch at a beach house. There is a loveseat with a small table beside it. On the table is a bud vase with a rose in it.

JEAN: (*She is seated on the loveseat.*) Your father was a right pain in the neck sometimes, Madeleine. I'm not going to lie about that . . . Oh, of course I was very angry about his affair. You're very naïve. You don't know what you would have done because you're not me. I did stand up to him, in my own way. And Barbara never entered the picture again. You grew up, and your father and I were very happy once again. There are things about our marriage you'll never understand, with your modern expectations about what a wife can demand from her husband. Maybe I shouldn't have told you all of this. I'm sorry I opened my mouth. I guess I just wanted you to know we had problems, that's all. And if you think I'm complacent, well, you try being married for thirty-nine years. You just try it. Nothing comes easy in life, my dear. I would like to have had more children. But it didn't work out that way; we made do with one. And as you know, your father took great pride in your achievements.

When you graduated, he was so pleased. He told me once he wanted you to marry a man who worships you, the way he did me. That's why I fell in love with him. Besides the fact that he was charming, he absolutely adored me. When I confronted him about his affair, he really was contrite. He had regrets about betraying our marriage. And really, the whole thing only lasted six months. You must remember that. (*There is a silence.*) Nothing in life works out just as you think it will. It wasn't easy afterwards. Those rose-colored glasses you wear when you're young begin to fade a little when you realize your husband has an eye for other women. The bitterness didn't go away quickly. But it did go away. We still had our holidays together, we had you, and of course he continued to remember our anniversaries for years after that. He always brought me flowers, or a pretty nightgown, or he took me out for dinner. And what I found was that, even when a marriage has been troubled, there is something nostalgic that remains of the past. Your father and I kept that something. I suppose you'd call it our early memories. (*She smooths her skirt over her knees and takes a rose from the bud vase on the table, twisting it between her fingers.*) And the next summer, when you were sixteen, we came back here to our cottage with you, and had a splendid summer. The tide kept bringing seashells in, and the lighthouse kept beaming through the fog at dusk. The seagulls still decorated the sky, the roses bloomed on the trellises, and the stars still gleamed when the sky grew dark at night. It was peaceful here, and I had begun to forgive him. You must remember that about forgiveness, Madeleine. The past, the good part of the past, is always with us. There is always something of it that remains.

JUICE

by Pat Montley

CHARACTER: WOMAN, early fifties

WOMAN: I was afraid I would dry up. Like the proverbial prune. They say women do, after menopause. But I haven't. Not yet anyway. (*Puzzled.*) The fact is, I feel . . . steamy. It's not the hot flashes—they've come and gone. This is different. I wake up in the middle of the night and my whole body is . . . moist. My palms and soles feel like the leaves of lush tropical plants. It's as though my heart is pumping electric currents into all my fluids. And at that moist moment, I feel a readiness—no, an . . . *urgency* . . . to do something . . . to be something . . . *more.* Something strange is happening. My pores are open. Things get in. Light, for example. It invades me. When I drive in the country on a bright morning, the sun passes through my flesh as easily as it passes through the car window. When I walk down the street on a sunny day, the light penetrates by body. I no longer cast a shadow. Last week, I went to a Monet exhibit and when I saw *Meadow at Giverny*, I felt I was the light in that meadow—that my breath was the breeze above that yellow green grass. People get in too. They steam open my pores and come right in. I was sitting in the park yesterday, watching a toddler try to get on her sister's tricycle. She tackled it from the front, from the side, and eventually from the back, until she sat precariously but triumphantly on the seat, listing slightly, her feet dangling above the pedals. And suddenly I was crying, heady with my success, for I had become that fearless child. I find now that my senses are more . . . *aroused*. By smells, for example. The leather conditioner I use on my boots . . . the crisp, glossy pages of a new book . . . the delicate spray of an orange as the skin is peeled . . . the warm, cloying scent of my own body as I bend over the breakfast counter in my nightgown. I'm more aware . . . more *appreciative*. Touching comforts me. I open to it. Nothing to hide, nothing to lose. I enjoy embracing my friends, pressing my body close to theirs, feeling the bulges of breasts and bellies, the sturdiness of thighs and shoulders, faces cradled in necks, inhaling affection like a fine perfume. Making love, I am surprised by passion flowing through me like a river of light. I know the dance by heart; yet still the music moves me deeply—until I sing and sing and flood the world with my delight.

LANGUAGE ROOMS

by Yussef El Guindi

CHARACTER: **SAMIR**, fifties or sixties. He is dressed in a gallebeya, and baseball cap

---

SAMIR: So my son one day says he is going to teach his father this great sport of baseball. I think he is embarrassed that I know so little about the great pastimes of our new home. So he tries to teach me. Very earnest, my son. All frowns up here as he tells me why this person does this, and why there are these (*Makes signals players might make.*) signals, and why the pitcher may do this, (*Touches his hat.*) or that; and why the coach might get so upset and scream in the face of the umpire. I thought soccer players had bad manners, but who chews tobacco in soccer? And how many times must a player touch himself before you feel he must see a doctor? Anyway. My son, the sportsman, he teach me. . . . (*Remembering, smiling.*) My son . . . He made something of himself, you know. I can say my son took his new home at its word and said yes, I'm in. I have arrived. This is my country. But—you see, for me—for those who just get here, it is more like—well, like baseball. At least what I understand of it. You hit the ball, and then you make a decision. Do I go for it? Take the chance? And I said yes. The letter came and we all said yes. (*Perhaps starts sketching in what he means, using the stage*

as an imagined baseball field.) Leave safety and go for opportunity.
And that's what it feels like; oh my God, exactly what it feels
like. Between two bases. You're in the world of running now.
You make it or too bad. Back home, you have the safety of
family, you have history, here? Who are you? You are nothing
except running and trying to make it. My wife and I, we say, one
day we will go back. But you can't. You have hit the ball and all
you're trying to do now is stay in the game. And you think,
Why? Why did we put ourselves in this position? And where—
where is all this milk and honey we were told was here? (*Slight
beat.*) But—I . . . I regret nothing.—You can tear yourself up
like that. I only wish in all this running I had spent more time
paying attention to my family. Because . . . I would've seen
what was happening. The changes—in my children. In my son
especially. Because one day suddenly from nowhere I see a look,
in his eyes. When I go to pick him up at school. Something I had
never seen before. And it was . . . embarrassment. For his father.
At this foreign-looking man who was picking him up in front
of the other kids. (*Slight beat.*) But you know what I thought
when I saw that look on him? I said good. He's fitting in. He's
the one out of all of us who's going to make it. He's going to
hit the home run and make it all the way round. He will be the
one good reason we came. (*Slight beat.*) No. Immigration, it is
not for sissies. You may change countries, move your body
across a border. But in here, (*Taps heart.*) where that travels to?
Where it settles, if it does—this is a much more complicated
road. The places the heart stops to find comfort—because it
must find comfort if it is to go on—those are not always good
places for the heart. (*Slight beat.*) The price for a better life,
you see . . . it is always a little higher than you think it will be.

MAKING GOD LAUGH

by Sean Grennan

CHARACTER: Thomas, fifties

THOMAS: Pop . . . do you have any idea how much I love being a priest? Every day I get up, and I know I've got something important to do. That people need me and I need them. I just put that other thing away, like I was supposed to. And then Helen came to volunteer. You think you know what you're doing in life and then. . . . She was nice, we laughed a few times, really that's it. And then once I found her crying in church. It was nothing, a thing with her boss. I comforted her, and she turned to me. She took my hand and looked at me and I didn't even hear what she was saying because this thing . . . this thing wasn't put away anymore. It got so quiet and I looked around at the church, and I could tell it was going to be different, I knew . . . right then. It even looked different, the candles, the pews, all looked familiar but like I was looking at an old picture, like walking past a house you used to live in. You know, pretty soon I'll be some story about a priest who "fell." That's how they'll say it, I "fell." And that's about right because it feels like gravity pulling me . . . I have to do it . . .

A TO Z

by Monica Raymond

CHARACTER: **MS. BEE**, seventy. African American

MS. BEE: Barack, now—that's like a miracle. I never thought to see this day. When we used to go down in the summer to see my mother's people in Carolina—the things I seen—And they don't tell you none of that in *Eyes on the Prize*! They say there was separate water fountains and bathrooms, but they don't tell you a lot of the stops there were no colored restrooms. And my big brother would say "Don't drink, don't drink," but I couldn't help it, I got so thirsty! And we'd be doing the bee dance, hopping from foot to foot. And at each station, "Is there a colored restroom?" and "No—dang it!" and the train'd just go on and on. We had to go so bad! One time I wet myself, and I just sitting there on that hard train seat all stinky, and my mother said "Aren't you ashamed?" But I couldn't help it. Must've been five, six hundred miles without a rest stop. Or felt like it, anyway. And now this! Barack. That is God's grace that I would live to see the day. Everybody so happy. And I'm the bad fairy at the picnic. On account of Jerome. Shot in the back. Just playing in the street. Five years old. My godson. Cutest thing. Just out playing, never did harm to nobody. Just caught in the crossfire. They say he's gonna be all right. Well, not all right, he's shot in the spine. Maybe he'll walk. Maybe he'll be some kind of plegic—paraplegic, quadriplegic. But they got metal now, they've got medical wonders—I've been reading. They implant a circuit and you spark yourself into life just by flicking your tongue.

MY FIRST PEDICURE

by Katherine Burkman

CHARACTER: ELLEN, seventy-two

CIRCUMSTANCE: Ellen is talking to her pedicurist in a beauty salon.

ELLEN: Oh, that tickles. That's alright, just go ahead. Pedicure away! (*Pause. She leans forward.*) My daughter insisted that I have this pedicure. I'm seventy-two, almost seventy-three, and it never even occurred to me to have such a procedure. Just in and out for haircuts, that's me. I only come to your salon because you people have been very nice to me. I'm attached. If I weren't, to be absolutely honest, I'd go someplace much cheaper and probably look more or less the same when I emerged. So a pedicure? Whatever for? One problem is that, as you see, my feet are ticklish. Another problem is they have not done well under the stress of too many pounds they've had to carry around for so many years. They were, even though I do say this myself, quite lovely when I was young and carefree. Then in middle age they began to bother me. Naturally, I blamed my shoes. Over and over again, I blamed my shoes. After about ten years of this, I went to a podiatrist and found out I had neuromas on top of each foot and bunions on the sides. Surgery was advised, but I have not taken that advice.

Since then, as you can see, one middle toe has risen above the others and is usually rather sore. I am, consequently, the little old lady in tennis shoes that one always reads about. That is all that I can bear to have on my feet, except at weddings and funerals. And not just any old sneakers. Running shoes. Not that I run, but they are the most padded. My daughter said all my worries about my feet showed my need for a pedicure. In fact, she made me promise to have one and then send her a picture. Well, I thought, I am into being good to myself. I can afford it. I think I can afford it. No money is really secure, so the thing to do is spend it. (*Pause. She recoils.*) Ouch. Don't worry, just sensitive. My daughter lives in San Francisco, which I guess is partly why she is so big on pedicures. The very name is a bit off-putting. If I didn't know better, I would think a pedicure was a treatment for pedophiles. I just think that nothing can cure what's wrong with my feet, so why bother. But I have one powerful daughter.

ON THE BRINK OF MIDDLE AGE

by Yvette Heyliger

CHARACTER: WOMAN, fifty, African American, dressed in a running suit

CIRCUMSTANCE: The play explores the mixed emotions of a woman who is in the process of entering a new stage of life and who, in a flash of insight, reclaims and redefines aging in the new millennium.

WOMAN: I admit it. I am slowly losing my "friend." The Change of Life is a process that can spread over thirteen years, the doctor said. I don't know how to respond; what to think of this impending loss; how to handle being, *perimenopausal*. I'm all rusting pipes and mixed metaphors about getting older. Thank God, I am a woman of color. We hold up well. Admirers bear this out: "Girl, you don't look like you have a daughter in college." Or my favorite; "You two could be sisters!" But, the truth is, I am on the brink of what? Saying goodbye to my monthly friend and hello to: having hot flashes, night sweats, and dizzy spells; adding bifocals to my eyeglass prescription; dying persistent grey hairs black; getting tracks of hair sewn into my scalp to make up for inevitable hair loss; propping up my sulking breasts in a padded bra; covering my "muffin top" with a loose-fitting cotton shirt, or stuffing myself into a girdle hoping to recreate some semblance a waistline; wearing sensible shoes with orthotics; taking estrogen or calcium supplements; *wondering at what point a lubricant will become necessary for sex?* Lucky me! I rip off my clothes and stand in front of the long mirror, looking at myself, *naked.* I turn around and look over my shoulder. I do have more junk in my trunk. I face forward . . . and under the hood too. Thank goodness for my pretty skin, good teeth, formerly-beautiful-now-handsome-face, and winning personality. And then I realize . . . all is not lost! Why, just the other day the talking head on the evening news declared, "Thirty is the new twenty and forty is the new thirty." I lace up and go out for a power walk. *There's no reason fifty can't be the new forty!*

PLAY MEMORY

by Joanna M. Glass

CHARACTER: CAM, approximately fifty, fifty-five years old, wears an old baggy sweater

CIRCUMSTANCE: The MacMillan home. Cam shuffles to the phone.

CAM: Hello? No, Jean's not here. Wait a minute . . . wait a minute! I have a sinking feeling that this call is settin' a precedent. I have a distinctly sinking feeling that I am speaking with a young person of the masculine gender. Arn I? (*He frowns.*) Oh, dear. What's your name? MacLeod. God, I've always hated that tartan. Plaid, man, tartan! The MacLeods have sported a putrid sort of tartan for several hundred years now. It's a kind of bilious yellow with great blobs of black. It is, in my considered opinion, the most undistinguished of Scottish tartans. If you don't mind my asking, MacLeod, what do you want with my Jeannie, as if I didn't know? (*He listens.*) Uh huh. Uh huh. Uh huh. Jean's fourteen, how old are you? Ah. Sixteen's a bad age. Horny all the time at sixteen. Listen, lad, I think what you really want is one of those floozies from the west side. Y'see, Jean's a member of the noble clan MacMillan. Yes. If there is any such thing as a Canadian aristocracy, we are it. (*Becoming irritated.*) Look, fish and chips and a hockey game is a lot of crap. What you're lookin' to do, MacLeod, is slip it to my Jeannie. And I won't have it. I'm old and battered. I've suffered more losses than you'll ever know gains. I'm dirt poor and I drink too much and my brain cells have run amok. (*Almost whispering, feigning begging.*) Please, lad, spare me. Don't saddle me with a bastard MacLeod in a putrid yellow tartan.

RICHIE

by Diana Amsterdam

CHARACTER: RICHIE, mid-fifties

CIRCUMSTANCE: On the phone, Richie is talking with his girlfriend. His side of the conversation is all that's heard, shifting from place to place, time to time.

RICHIE: I do make you a priority, you're right after my photography and my mother, no, not right after, you're right up there. Baby, I'm doing the best I can. You need to trust that. I can't give you any more time than I do, you've got to trust that I'm doing my best. I love you. Okay? (*Beat, change setting.*) I hear you and I am too, I wish my life wasn't such a bitch and I could spend more time but for now, we have our Saturday night and Sunday day (*Listens.*) Sunday morning, and Wednesday night dinner together (*Listens.*) right, you do always come to me and you've been really great about keeping it linear, just the two hours in the hood because that's all the time I've (*Listens.*) baby, you've got to trust me, okay? I love you, when will you hear that, and I'm doing the best I can, don't you think I wish I had more time, for myself, for my mother, my work, and for you, you're right up there, you've got to trust me, okay? I love you, baby, you know that, right? (*Beat, change setting.*) This, okay this is, you need to listen to, really hear this, this isn't about whether I've got time for us, I do have time for us I make time for us although it's not always easy, do you know how tired I am tonight? But here I am with you anyway, right? I'm doing the best I can, giving you all the time I can and you. Have. To. Trust me, tell me you fucking trust me. (*Listens.*) Thank you baby. I love you. I. Love. You. and you've got to trust me on this, this isn't about how I feel or don't feel about you, or whether I have time for a relationship, or whether I'm still married or any of that shit, this is about my life and how tough it is and you've got to trust me, I'm doing the best I can.

THE KILLER AND THE COMIC

by Andy Rooster Bloch

CHARACTER: BARNEY, sixties

BARNEY: So get this. Me and Mort. We're flying down Route 22. I'm talkin' fifty miles an hour. So I says, Mort. For Chrisake, slow down. Nah, he says. I run these roads for years. I know every turn, every twig, every bump from here to Buffalo. So he doesn't slow down. Not even a kilometer per second. I don't know metric from gonorrhea, but I know we're near Canada. Trust me on his one. So I says, Mort. You schmuck. You lymph node on the ass of a gibbon. There's enough ice on this fakakta road to make Ethiopia a skating rink. He still doesn't slow down. All of a sudden, a fog blankets the street and he loses all visibility. He cuts it to the left, to the right. He makes every move but the hokey-pokey and the next thing you know, we're two balding Jews careening off the road in a rented Lexus. Which, by the way, ain't a bad car. Mort's got a brother in Albany that sets him up. Personally, I can't stand the fat bastard. Not Mort, his brother. Where was I? Oh yeah. So we fly off the road into a guard rail. We get a flat. I says, Mort. Goddamit. Look what you've done. We got two shows tomorrow night at the Buffalo Sheraton. And instead of goin' through the act, we gotta play Jeremiah Szedrate and Grizzly Schmuck in some backwoods, blizzard-filled, bullshit landfill. So I says, I'm gonna call for help. You're the putz that got us into this mess, so you change the fakakta tire. I pointed to your cabin and said meet me at Abe Lincoln's wooden wet dream in twenty minutes. So tell me. You gotta phone?

THE SECRET WISDOM OF TREES

by Christine Toy Johnson

CHARACTER: DANNY, a youthful eighty-one

CIRCUMSTANCE: Danny reminisces about the first time he met his beloved Abby, now failing from Alzheimer's.

DANNY: It was colder than most Septembers that year, and I had left my dorm again with only a sweater on, some horrible thing that my Mother had thrown in my suitcase just to spite me for saying I was "too much of a man now" to ever get cold. And here comes this tiny, wild gust of wind, her chestnut brown hair, this glorious mane of good sense whipping through the air at me. "Here. I made this for you. I can't stand looking at you shivering in that stupid sweater any more. So wear it in good health." And she hands me this lumpy, hand-knit burgundy scarf—crooked stitches, fringes finished as if she'd torn the yarn off with her own teeth—and the most beautiful thing I'd ever seen. I married her four years later to the day. I've kept the scarf all these years, too. (*He smiles.*) I don't know what my life would be without her. I don't want to know. Oh, we've had our bumps. An empty bank account here, a terrifying health scare there. But she's never given up on me. Or the idea that we could be a family, no matter how big or small. Or the idea that we could get by on the kind of tenacity you develop only over the passage of fifty or sixty winters together, huddled under a series of decreasingly threadbare blankets. That callus you build up as a united front against complete and utter despair when nothing turns out the way you thought it would—and the wings you sprout together when everything sails far beyond your wild expectations. Because at the end of the day, there's this incredible, still tiny, still wild, still most beautiful gust of wind I've ever seen who takes my breath away and says, "I love you, Danny Green." I mean, what else in the world could possibly matter? (*He takes a deep breath.*) Still. We could never be prepared for . . . all of *this*.

WHERE'S JULIE?

by Daniel Guyton

CHARACTER: MOM, fifties

CIRCUMSTANCE: Mom has just learned that her fifteen-year-old daughter Julie is pregnant, and considering an abortion. Mom addresses Julie's boyfriend, Hector.

MOM: Oh my! You smell like marijuana! (*Beat.*) I haven't smelled that since I was a girl. You know, Hector, Julie's father and I were in love at a young age, too. Well, I was young anyway. He was older. I mean, he wasn't twenty-two! But, he was . . . older. He was about twenty or so. And I loved him. Oh, he was so handsome. And this was during the seventies, so he was kind of a pothead. And I thought that was dangerous. It excited me! I came from a very conservative family, and so this was wild. Rebellious! And my parents warned me day in and day out that I should stay away from him. That he was the devil and he would lead me into temptation! Well, I wasn't having any of that. No sir! So, I just went right ahead and had my fun. And one night . . . Well . . . (*Whispering.*) We had the sex. Oh boy, was it ever good, but . . . sure enough, I got pregnant. Julie's father wanted me to abort, but my parents wanted none of that! They made me get married. And I did, and it was OK at first. I was so in love with him. I still am, I suppose. We had three children, me and Harold. And we *are* still married today, so I guess that says something. But those drugs he did just . . . scrambled his brains like a cat in a blender! It's like a big fog surrounds him day in and day out. He doesn't know where he is sometimes. He can't . . . work, he can't make his own breakfast! He's helpless! He's a big baby! And I want to leave him, Hector! I want to leave him, but I can't! Because I love him! Do you see what I'm saying?!

SCENES

A BODY OF WATER

by Neena Beber

CHARACTERS: MARGUERITE and JOE, middle-aged

CIRCUMSTANCE: Marguerite and Joe recline at the beach. They start off playing teenagers.

MARGUERITE: I look fat. Do I look fat?

JOE: No.

MARGUERITE: Look at me. I'm so fat. This bathing suit makes me look fat. Admit it. I'm, like, totally bloated. I just—uchh—it's disgusting.

JOE: You're not fat.

MARGUERITE: (*Of unseen passerby:*) Do I look like that? I look like that, right?

JOE: You spend too much time focusing on the physical.

MARGUERITE: Well it's the beach. We're at the beach.

JOE: I'll bet you spend eighty percent of your waking time focused on your physical presence in the world. Does it matter? Will it? Ultimately?

MARGUERITE: Are you saying this because I look fat?

(She stands and steps forward.)

Years later I develop a conscience, a strong moral fiber, an interest in social justice. I march for human rights; I march against fur; I march for humanitarian efforts abroad; I march against hunger; I march for the environment; I march for Palestinians, Bosnians, Hindus, Pakistanis, Sri Lankans, Peruvians, Christians, non-believers, Jews; I chain myself to a tree, to a wall, to a tractor; I am sent to prison for a short time; I am stabbed in prison; I survive; the scar gets darker over time before it fades.

(Goes back to sunning; of her own flesh:)

This should not be here. I'm supposed to be in the prime of my youth, the full bloom or whatever. Most people don't even have to exercise until they're way into their like twenties or something, and look at me, I'm already—I hate this.

JOE: This is why it makes sense to cover. Not just to protect you from the temptation of others, but to protect you from the temptation from yourself to think only of surfaces. To protect yourself from the judgment of others and of yourself. A physical barrier frees you from physical limitations.

MARGUERITE: You're saying this because I look fat. Are you? Some people look really good in bathing suits and some people don't. It's not like your thoughts are so deep. I mean, are you even going to go to college, Joe?

JOE: Not everyone gets to go to college.

MARGUERITE: But you're smart. You could.

JOE: Well gee, thanks, but you're not the one who makes the decisions. I don't think you understand how things work. The tides—do you even understand how the tides work?

MARGUERITE: I don't know. Gravity. Or something. The full moon?

JOE: There are forces bigger than us, that's all I'm saying. Years later I return to the Germany of my grandparents. I am searching for the synagogue where my grandfather prayed. I am searching for the marzipan factory. I am searching for the ancestral home. Years later I have this need to return to a place I never knew. Do you want to go in the water?

MARGUERITE: You're so skinny.

JOE: I'm not skinny.

MARGUERITE: I wish I were skinny like you.

JOE: Guys don't exactly want to get called "skinny" if you want to get into that. Which I don't. I really like the beach. I like to come here and think. Don't ruin that for me. I like to watch the waves.

MARGUERITE: There aren't even any waves today. No big ones, anyway, none you can ride. It's so calm. Years later, I find myself at a train station after my divorce, which is bitter and protracted. I have an existential crisis. I travel widely. I come to understand my mother. Years later, I cry at such simple things. Are you going to try to ride the waves today? Joe? I'll bet your thoughts aren't that deep. I'll bet underneath it all they aren't any deeper than mine.

JOE: I miss the beach.

MARGUERITE: How can you miss it when we're right here?

JOE: I don't know. Years later I develop arthritis, diverticulitis, gallstones, mild diabetes, and an enlarged prostate. I pee night and day and I can't take a shit. I have an affair with a younger woman. Her skin is so plain and smooth that I weep.

MARGUERITE: God. I hope I don't get that old. I can't imagine it. Can you imagine—us? No way. They'll probably have things they can do to keep it all together by then, right?

ALABAMA BOUND

by Charlotte Higgins

CHARACTERS: LORETTA and DONALD, middle aged

CIRCUMSTANCE: At a critical point in Loretta's life, she is trying to cope with living with her under-employed husband Donald and her tyrannical mother-in-law, Noonie.

LORETTA: I heard on the news that six hundred people died up in Chicago last week from the heat. Mostly old people, laying there dead all by theirselves. Been over 100 degrees down here ten days in a row. Noonie keeps it freezing in here. Guess she's afraid they'll find her dead like those other old people. Noonie's my mother-in-law. Donald, her son, is my husband.

Donald's home from work. He's sitting in the living room in his recliner. Noonie's sitting over there in her matching recliner. A pitcher of iced tea sets on the table between them, next to Noonie's ashtray. That table's all scarred with water stains and burns from Noonie's cigarettes. My mama gave me that table thirty years ago as a wedding present. Them two's watching *Entertainment Tonight*; gray light's flickering on their faces, making them look kinda slack-jawed.

Oh, my, Mary Hart's looking all serious. Oh. They're showing that Christmas home video of those two babies that Susan Smith drowned. Now they put two 900 telephone numbers up on the screen. You call one 900 number if you want Susan Smith executed. You call the other one if you just want her to rot in prison.

Noonie grabs a pencil and turns on the lamp beside her; the one with the shade still wrapped in plastic. The one she bought eight years ago, when I was in the Baptist Hospital having my hysterectomy. Noonie writes down the number, stabs out her cigarette and takes a gasp of air from the little green tank that sets on the floor beside her. Now she punches in the numbers on the blue princess telephone and says EXECUTION! Donald punches in the same numbers. She tells me to call.

"In the kitchen, Noonie. Dinner's almost done."

I walk that narrow vinyl runner that cuts through the middle of the living room. Noonie put it there to save the shag carpeting she had installed four years ago, when I was in the Baptist Hospital having my hysterectomy.

In the kitchen I pick up the telephone. I call in. Hang up. Call in. Hang up. Call in. Hang up. By the time I'm finished, I've cancelled out their two executions and added six more to the life in prison total.

I look around the kitchen at Noonie's dinette set, Noonie's teapot clock, and Noonie's favorite dinner setting on the stove—salmon croquettes, mashed potatoes, and Le Sueur

English peas. And I wonder: Is execution really worse than life in prison?

Then I put some extra salt in the Le Sueurs, even though I know it'll make Noonie's breathing harder tonight. Donald tramps into the kitchen now to get more ice for the tea.

DONALD: Execute the bitch!

LORETTA: He used to not talk like that. Started talking like that when he got laid off as manager of the County Bank. A big New York Bank came through these parts buying up all the little banks, like Sherman marching through Georgia. They laid Donald off eighteen months before he could draw his pension. Took him two years to find a new job— changing oil at Quicky Lube.

DONALD: Dinner done? Noonie's hungry.

LORETTA: Yes, Donald, I fixed her favorite.

DONALD: Croquettes! You had croquettes night before last, Loretta! Where's your mind?

LORETTA: He takes out a cigarette. Donald, you can't smoke in here. The kitchen is mine. (*Pauses.*) I went to see the doctor this morning. I'm going in for surgery again. They may cut off my other breast. I think maybe at this point, your Mama'd be better off in a convalescent home.

DONALD: Loretta, she'd rather die than go in a convalescent home.

LORETTA: She's had that opportunity and passed it up.

DONALD: She pays the utilities and buys all the groceries.

LORETTA: I'll get a job!

DONALD: Doing what? You're old and ain't got no skills, Loretta!

LORETTA: Donald, I can't stand her in the house anymore.

DONALD: Loretta, don't start.

LORETTA: Donald, it's either her or me.

DONALD: Loretta, I don't know what you want.

LORETTA: I want something different before I die.

DONALD: She's waiting on her tea.

LORETTA: Donald, you walk away from me now, and it's over. (*Long pause.*) Never noticed how much his pants bagged in the butt.

BEAUTIFUL CLEAR-EYED WOMAN

by Diana Amsterdam

CHARACTERS: THEODORA, fifty-five; FRANNY, fifty

CIRCUMSTANCE: Theodora is paying an unexpected visit to Franny's house in the Berkshires. She is Franny's sister-in-law. Theodora's daughter has recently run away.

FRANNY: Can I get you something? Coffee. Black, no sugar, right?

THEODORA: Cream. Lots of sugar.

(FRANNY *exits to kitchen.* THEODORA *sits on couch. Glances impatiently towards kitchen.*)

(THEODORA *talks to kitchen.*) Yes, I'm here to conduct my own personal Lisa quest. Frank, of course, has hired a detective but that's a big fat bust, and now he emails me that he's gonna fly around in his Supercub, no doubt playing hero to that big bosom bland he married.

(THEODORA *finds leopard-skin panties under a couch cushion. She stares at them, stuffs them back into the couch.* FRANNY *returns with coffee and a donut.*)

FRANNY: I don't have cream. Ice cream okay?

(FRANNY *hands the coffee mug to* THEODORA *who regards it dubiously.*)

THEODORA: So I hear you got your novel published! Congratulations.

FRANNY: Unfortunately. That didn't happen.

THEODORA: It didn't? I'm sorry.

FRANNY: They said they were gonna publish it but they lied. The head dog showed it to his wife, his *wife*. And she didn't like my heroine. She didn't like my heroine! So I chew that for a while and decide I'll talk to the editor, but she won't answer my calls. I finally get her and she gives me this idiot rap about the new female ideal, she's a warrior, she can't afford to get infected by people, infected by people? And I say, politely, is it good for women writers if we can only write one kind of woman? Men aren't restricted, so why should we be? And she says it's up to you and hangs up.

THEODORA: Yes, I can see that would be difficult for you. Gentle Franny, always infected by someone.

(*Beat of silence.*)

FRANNY: You still do that. Suddenly swipe your claws along my throat.

THEODORA: For better or worse, my claws have only gotten sharper.

FRANNY: Well, don't use them on me. My skin has gotten thinner.

THEODORA: You're not having a donut?

FRANNY: I'm on a diet.

FRANNY: So, no, but go ahead.   **THEODORA:** Of course you are.

THEODORA: I, on the other hand, am on an anti-diet. Do you see I've put on a few pounds?

FRANNY: No.

THEODORA: I'm allowing myself to take up more space in the world, I'm allowing myself to have volume. I was always starving myself for Frank because Frank likes his women skinny. But I could never be quite skinny enough and then I got older and he left me! It was inevitable. Frank can't live without his image of himself and his image is a man who has the best of everything including the best tits and ass.

FRANNY: Probably a reflection on the size of his dick. Look, I don't blame you for being furious at Frank, we're all furious at him, I've hardly spoken to him since my father died, everybody agrees Frank is the villain and he is the villain but well, you know. Frank needs to have the biggest the best the first, because he's got an empty hole where . . .

FRANNY (*Cont'd*): his confidence   **THEODORA:** Don't defend him should be.   to me.

THEODORA: Don't defend him! He tossed out his wife of twenty-five years so he could fuck a hat-check girl, and he managed, in the six short months he had responsibility for our daughter, to alienate her to push her away, and now she's pregnant, now Lisa is pregnant!

FRANNY: Lisa is pregnant?

THEODORA: And homeless. She says she's living out of a car but I don't know if that's true, I don't know . . .

| THEODPRA (*Cont'd*): what she's eating | FRANNY: You're in touch with her? |

THEODORA: Or how she's surviving. (*Takes postcards out of her bag.*) She sends me postcards from Seattle, from Denali, I get a card from her nearly every day but I think they may be fakes, they're all alike, and she is so creative, she'd draw things, she'd write poems, she would never send me these boring look-alikes.

(FRANNY *takes the cards, eyes them.*)

FRANNY: These are real postcards, I know . . .

| FRANNY (*Cont'd*): I used to work in the post office. | THEODORA: I know they're real postcards. |

THEODORA: I'm saying she didn't send them!

| FRANNY: Well then who else? | THEODORA: I think Lisa is here. |

FRANNY: Here? You think your daughter is here?

THEODORA: She always adored you, free-spirited Aunt Franny, yes, I think she's here somewhere, I think you're hiding her from me.

(*Blackout. End of scene.*)

.

BITTEN

by Penny Jackson

CHARACTERS: BRIAN, young; STELLA, seventy-five

CIRCUMSTANCE: In a New York City Irish pub, Brian, a young doctor, confronts his grandmother, Stella, about moving to an assisted living home. Stella is reluctant to leave the New York City Irish pub she calls her home.

STELLA: You've seen dead people, yes? In medical school? What do they look like?

BRIAN: They look dead.

STELLA: That's right. They're quiet. They're asleep. That's not such a bad thing.

BRIAN: But I don't want you to die. So please, stop drinking. Move to Sunset House. Pretend it's called Sunrise if it makes you feel happier.

STELLA: Aren't you going to tell me that you love me?

BRIAN: You know I love you, Grandma.

STELLA: And I love you too, Brian. You're my favorite grandchild.

BRIAN: I'm your only grandchild!

STELLA: You still look at me. Most people try not to see me. I remind them. I remind them of the future. You can smell an old person a mile away. I don't stink, do I?

BRIAN: Of course not.

STELLA: I still wear your grandfather's favorite perfume. Chanel Number 5, though I can barely afford it. Made Frank crazy. But love like that can't last forever, can it?

BRIAN: I don't know.

STELLA: It has to burn out like a candle. Frank and I thought it would burn 450 degrees every night. That's something you learn. It's not the easiest lesson. That's why you need someone who will be there for you. Even when you look like me now.

(The jukebox begins to play "Danny Boy." STELLA suddenly stops.)

Listen.

BRIAN: "Danny Boy"? Wasn't that.

STELLA: Your grandfather's favorite song. Doesn't matter how many times I hear it, I think of him and I want to cry.

BRIAN: He sang it every morning when he drove me to school.

(STELLA begins to sing.)

STELLA: O Danny Boy, the pipes, the pipes are calling

From glen to glen, and down the mountainside.
The summer's gone and all the roses falling . . .

(STELLA *begins to cry.*)

Oh, your poor grandfather. He had a terrible death.

BRIAN: I know.

STELLA: His body so stiff that he couldn't even raise his pinky. And then the dementia. Howling at night like a wolf.

BRIAN: I'm sorry that Grandpa suffered so.

STELLA: Still, after all those years, it hurts. You think the pain fades away but it doesn't. Not when you love someone. Even after they're gone, and you're almost gone, you still remember. Do you understand what I'm saying?

BRIAN: Yes I do. That's why I won't fall in love again.

STELLA: Sure you will. But Brian, first you got to forgive. You got to forgive. When you get to my age, you start to forgive everyone. You got to forgive Pedro. You got to forgive your mother. Brian, you can change.

BRIAN: You can change too. Move to a new place. Make new friends. Have people take care of you.

STELLA: I'm scared to go to that home!

BRIAN: Gran, please don't cry.

STELLA: Why can't I just stay here at The Dublin Rose with my friends and "Danny Boy" always on the jukebox? This is my home, my neighborhood. This is where I want to watch my sun set.

BRIAN: I wish you could stay too. But you can't live here anymore. It's too dangerous. You'll get hurt.

STELLA: But I don't want to be with old people. See, when I wake up every morning, I don't think I look like this. I think I look like, oh, I guess, when I was twenty-one. Don't know why, but I do. So it's always a shock to see my breasts no longer so perky, and my arms and legs looking like broken-down limbs. And my face. Oh dear. I look at myself in the mirror and think, the mirror must have cracked. There's no way, Stella, you could have so many lines on your face.

BRIAN: You're still beautiful to me.

STELLA: Ah, but you would have to say that, wouldn't you?

BLACK FOREST

by Anthony Giardina

CHARACTERS: HOMER, mid- to late sixties, **FRANK**, early to mid-sixties, **JACOB**, forties

CIRCUMSTANCE: The office of Jacob, a university administrator. Homer and Frank are professors at the university. Homer has been accused of inappropriately touching a student and will soon go before a committee.

HOMER: Frank, the Committee's decision's been put off to late in May. About me, I mean.

FRANK: Yes. It has.

HOMER: Why, Frank?

FRANK: It was felt—

HOMER: I don't like sentences in the passive voice. Someone felt. Some individual felt. And talked others into. Let's be straight.

FRANK: All of us on the Committee felt it's far too sensitive an issue to deal with during the school year. It would distract the students.

HOMER: So May. *Late May.*

FRANK: When the students are gone, yes.

HOMER: When those who might stand up in my defense are gone, anyway. I'm dead then, is what you're saying.

FRANK: We all have open minds, Homer. However, I feel it's only fair to warn you there are passionate people on this committee.

(JACOB *enters, carrying two cups of tea.*)

JACOB: Here we are. Nice hot—Where is she?

HOMER: She's dropping the Independent.

(JACOB *looks out into the hall for* WENDY. *Too late.*)

I'll take my tea, Jacob.

JACOB: She just left? Did she leave a message?

FRANK: Jacob, I'd like to talk to you.

HOMER: Finish, Frank. Passionate people.

FRANK: Yes, well, you know how hot an issue this has become. Time was, if a man was a good man, and tried to fondle a tit from time to time, nothing was done about it. A slap of the hand, if that.

HOMER: The Women have come into power, yes.

FRANK: (*As if this pains him.*) I will try to make every argument in your defense that I possibly can.

HOMER: (*Sipping his tea.*) And will you talk about the tits you've fondled, Frank?

FRANK: (*Beat.*) I don't think so.

HOMER: That ridiculous pregnancy how many years back?

FRANK: Many.

HOMER: Everyone knew about it. Still, you weren't punished.

FRANK: No, I wasn't. It's stupid to say I suffered, of course. But I did. Still, I wasn't punished. It would be hypocritical of me to bring in the word unfairness here.

HOMER: Good for you. Bloody good for you. Yes, the air is full of fine sentiments this morning. What I want to know is, what are any of you going to do about it?

FRANK: We are—sorry, I am going to argue as vehemently in your favor as I possibly can.

(FRANK *clears his throat.* HOMER *does a mock double-take.*)

I'm not against you, I find. I don't know how these others feel, but all of this puritanical nonsense seems to me a grand distraction from our true business, which some people seem to have forgotten is to educate. Against what might be a part of my better judgment, I find myself your advocate on the Committee.

HOMER: (*Has to take a moment just to take this in.*) Well, bravo, Yes, bravo.

FRANK: Now if you don't mind, I'd like to talk to Jacob alone.

HOMER: Oh, I don't mind. You're speaking the truth, are you?

FRANK: I am.

HOMER: (*Still with a grain of suspicion.*) I'm trusting you, Frank.

FRANK: I'm aware of that.

HOMER: But about the May decision—

FRANK: (*Firm.*) I can argue for you in Committee. I can't help you with the time. Just—sweat it out.

HOMER: (*Something occurs to him.*) Sweat it out. Yes. Thanks for the tea, Jacob. (*He exits.*)

JACOB: You shameless hussy. Every word of that was a lie, wasn't it?

FRANK: Every word, I'm afraid.

BREEDERS

by Bob Ost

CHARACTERS: **CARL LINDSTROM**, mid-sixties; **LEE FREDERICKS**, thirtyish

CIRCUMSTANCE: Carl is a sculptor and founder of The Heller Foundation. An absolute pillar of his community, or at least he'd like to think so, and damn anyone who thinks otherwise. Ruthless when necessary. Sometimes when it's not. Lee is Carl's secretary. Former actor, turned playwright at Carl's suggestion. Flamboyant. Excessive. Fun-loving? Don't believe it. Really not too fond of himself.

CARL: You're late.

LEE: I had trouble waking up.

CARL: Did you have an energetic night?

LEE: I walked Rita home, then Rick and I talked way into the wee hours.

CARL: How much longer will he be staying with you?

LEE: (*Annoyed.*) You know perfectly well that he's here for the week.

CARL: Fine. These need to be typed.

LEE: More rejections?

CARL: We can't afford to house every struggling artist who comes knocking at our door.

LEE: I feel sorry for them.

CARL: Then it's a good thing I make the decisions.

LEE: (*Starting to leave with letters.*) I'll go play evil fairy, spreading misery and disappointment for you.

(*Daintily tossing a letter at a time, like the Wicked Witch.*)

You're fucked! And you're fucked! And your little dog, too! What a world! What a world!

CARL: Conrad called a little while ago. They're closing your play.

LEE: (*Pause.*) What happened? I thought it was doing all right.

CARL: Don't waste time dwelling on it. Just finish your new one, and don't get side-tracked with experiments.

LEE: (*Pause.*) I'm sorry the play lost money.

CARL: We'll survive. There's always a market out there for Carl Lindstrom sculpture.

LEE: Doesn't it ever frustrate you? You knock them out, they eat them up. It seems too easy.

CARL: There's nothing easy about it. It's taken every bit of thirty years to perfect my technique, and to earn respect and a following.

LEE: But where's the challenge? It's the same damned thing over and over.

CARL: I'm a skilled craftsman. And as for challenge, I have quite enough keeping the Heller Foundation alive and functioning.

LEE: (*Pause, then as Tallulah.*) Well, dah-ling! I certainly didn't mean to touch any sore spots.

(*His own voice:*)

Speaking of sore spots, I woke up with the strangest pain in my right arm.

CARL: Why should this morning be any different?

LEE: Don't you see a lump?

CARL: Yes, but it's much farther down.

(CARL *grabs* LEE's *crotch.*)

LEE: (*Pulling away, as Tallulah.*) I'm dying of cancer, and you're making improper advances. That's practically necrophilia!

CARL: I need those letters typed, and some follow-up calls about the next exhibit. Not too heavy on John's paintings this time.

LEE: But he sells.

CARL: There's no accounting for taste. If he does one more blazing orange and black abstract, I might scream.

LEE: Why must everyone create according to Lindstrom's rules?

CARL: I never force my opinions on anyone. But maybe if I did, the forty-five artists living here wouldn't be supported by the work of only a handful of us.

LEE: A Mauree goes for five thousand and up.

CARL: This month. Fads die, and I'm not certain he has a strong enough technique to fall back on.

LEE: (*Pause, as Mae.*) From the way he was working on Rick, I'd say his technique is just fine.

CARL: Like I said before, there's no accounting for taste.

LEE: What do you have against Rick?

CARL: I don't think he belongs here.

LEE: Aren't you even going to submit his application to the board?

CARL: Come here.

LEE: What for?

CARL: What do you think? I haven't had you in two days. Not with your breeder friend here all the time.

LEE: Rick is not a breeder! He has no intention of having children. He just needs a place to live and work.

CARL: Now that he's unemployed and struggling, he's willing to take advantage of what we offer. Give him a little success, and he'll be out of here in no time, breeding with the rest of them.

LEE: All right, Carl. The world is a "sorry and meager place to live." It's diseased and hostile and shows no signs of improving. We all agree. But you can't expect every socially conscious person to be homosexual.

CARL: We'll talk later. Take off your pants.

LEE: I have typing to do.

CARL: It can keep.

LEE: You have no right.

CARL: Why do you suppose you're here?

LEE: I'm supposed to be your secretary.

CARL: There are hundreds of boys, younger and prettier than you, who would gladly do my typing. There might even be some who can type.

LEE: Not now.

CARL: Don't forget where I found you. I can send you right back. Take off your pants.

(LEE *stands motionless for a moment, then slowly walks towards* CARL. LEE *begins to undo his pants.*)

CLEANING HOUSE

by Marj O'Neill-Butler

CHARACTERS: **BILLIE**, seventy-four, a classy older woman; **MARCIA**, fifties, Billie's daughter; **BRAD**, sixty-five, Billie's friend

CIRCUMSTANCE: In their expensive home, Marcia is trying to get her mother, who has recently had a fall, to move into an assisted living complex. Billie, the mother, wants no part of it as she has found a new life. Marcia is in for more than one surprise after Brad enters the scene.

(BILLIE *is seated with her arm in a sling.* MARCIA *is pacing around the room.*)

BILLIE: Will you sit down. I can't stand you hovering. Hover, hover. I'm fine.

MARCIA: Mom, you fell. You could have broken something.

BILLIE: I didn't. It's just a sprain. Knock it off.

MARCIA: I think you need to listen to us.

BILLIE: I told you, I'm not moving to that place.

MARCIA: Mom, you could make friends there.

BILLIE: When have you ever seen me with a bunch of women? I don't like them. Boring. This aches. That aches. Gossip, gossip. Open a book, you stupid twit.

MARCIA: Well there are men there too.

BILLIE: If you can call them that. I don't want to live with old people. They bore me. Walkers. Wheelchairs. Canes. If I get like that, shoot me.

MARCIA: Mom, you are like that. You're seventy-four with a sprained shoulder.

BILLIE: Everything else works. Including my brain. Too bad you didn't inherit that from me.

MARCIA: Thanks, Mom. I'm just trying to do what's best for you.

BILLIE: Leave me be. That's what's best.

MARCIA: I promised Charles I'd try to get you to see reason.

BILLIE: Well, you failed. This is my house. I have my friends. I'm not going anywhere.

MARCIA: What friends? You just buried the last one a few weeks ago.

BILLIE: She wasn't a friend. She just filled in for bridge when we needed her.

MARCIA: Jeez, Mom.

BILLIE: Are you through?

MARCIA: You trying to get rid of me?

BILLIE: Not in so many words.

MARCIA: Then give me the words.

BILLIE: I'm expecting someone.

MARCIA: A guest? Who? From the Senior Center.

BILLIE: No, of course not. I don't go there. I told you. Too many old people.

MARCIA: Who then?

BILLIE: A friend.

MARCIA: Where did you meet this friend?

BILLIE: Not that it's any of your business, but Starbucks.

MARCIA: Since when do you drink coffee?

BILLIE: You are a bit behind, aren't you.

MARCIA: What?

BILLIE: Starbucks has more than coffee. Have you tried the chai frappé? It's really good.

MARCIA: Tell me about this friend. How old is she?

BILLIE: He. In his sixties.

MARCIA: Oh my God. (*Beat.*) Has he talked to you about your finances?

BILLIE: Wow, you get right to the point don't you. Yes. And he's given me good advice.

MARCIA: Like "give me some of your money and I'll invest it in my account." Mom, for a smart woman you are pretty stupid.

BILLIE: Thanks for that. As if you're the brightest spark plug in the universe.

MARCIA: Have you talked to Charles about this?

BILLIE: It's none of his business, or yours.

MARCIA: Of course it is. We don't want anyone taking advantage of you.

BILLIE: Why? You want my money for yourself? So you can shop 'til you drop? Again.

MARCIA: Pardon me?

BILLIE: Why do you think your husband left you? Not for another woman. Or a man. But because you have no idea about money, how much you waste, and how hard people work for it.

MARCIA: Yes I do.

BILLIE: When was your last job? And being a "trend whore" doesn't count. When have you ever worked for a living?

I'll tell you. Never. So don't go talking to me about money. It's mine and I earned it.

MARCIA: He could be after your money. You should really watch out for this man.

BILLIE: No more than you. And he's already made me forty grand this year.

MARCIA: How?

BILLIE: By investing in some good markets. How else?

(*The doorbell rings.*)

MARCIA: Is that him?

BILLIE: Yes. Do something useful and get the door.

(Marcia *leaves the room, and from offstage:*)

MARCIA: Brad! Hi! Come on in.

(*She reenters with Brad.*)

Brad Cooper's here from the Club! (*She smiles and flirts with Brad.*)

BILLIE: Yes dear, I know.

BRAD: Hello love. Sorry to hear about your shoulder. Put these in a vase will you?

(*He hands flowers to Marcia, who stares at both of them.*)

Close your mouth Marcia. You're about to drool.

DEAD AND BREATHING

by Chisa Hutchinson

CHARACTERS: CAROLYN, sixty-eight; VERONIKA, late thirties, her aide

CIRCUMSTANCE: A surprising conversation in Carolyn's elegant home.

VERONIKA: Okay, I get it. You're rich, I'm poor, joke's on me. Ha ha. You can stop fucking with me now.

CAROLYN: Why does everyone think I'm f—. My lawyer said the same thing when I called him to change my will.

VERONIKA: . . . You called your lawyer?

CAROLYN: Yes.

VERONIKA: When?

CAROLYN: When you were making me that tasty fucking omelet.

VERONIKA: You changed your will?

CAROLYN: Yes. Veronika-with-a-K Fern-like-the-plant is now my sole beneficiary.

VERONIKA: Beneficiary of what?

CAROLYN: A lady never discloses her net worth. Suffice it to say you could adopt a small army of children and never need a single cent of scholarship money to put them through college.

(*Pause.* VERONIKA *looks doubtful.* CAROLYN *picks up the phone and holds it out to* VERONIKA.)

Call my lawyer if you don't believe me. Just hit redial and ask for Martin. They'll try to tell you he's in an important meeting—just be insistent. He's probably sitting at his desk with his pants around his ankles, jerking off to internet porn. I actually caught him at it once. He's an excellent lawyer, but the man's got an addiction. Doesn't help that his wife's got a tundra between her legs. Frigid bitch. You know, I'm really starting to like that I can just say this kind of stuff around you. There aren't many people I can talk to like this.

(VERONIKA *stands and starts to walk away.*)

VERONIKA: Okay, crazy lady. I'm going to clean out your tub now.

CAROLYN: Eighty-seven million.

(VERONIKA *stops in her tracks.*)

Give or take a few hundred thousand. I don't have anyone else to give it to. You wouldn't be competing with any children or ambitious young gigolos. Martin gets three percent, but otherwise it's all yours.

(VERONIKA *turns back to* CAROLYN.)

The thing about a will, though . . . somebody's got to die for it to kick in.

(*Pause.*)

VERONIKA: Wow, I was so wrong. You're not Skywalker. You're Vader. You're bribing me now?

CAROLYN: I'm offering incentive.

VERONIKA: Eighty-seven million?

CAROLYN: That's not even counting the house. This wouldn't be such a bad place to raise a few kids.

VERONIKA: Oh sure. "And this is the room where I killed sweet old Ms. Carolyn so that I could inherit everything we have today, kids . . . "

CAROLYN: So sell it. Burn it. Whatever. I won't care, I'll be dead.

VERONIKA: You're serious.

CAROLYN: As AIDS.

VERONIKA: . . . That's fucked up.

CAROLYN: Well, we can't all pull off jokes about deadly diseases with the same aplomb as you.

VERONIKA: Just so I'm clear: you're telling me that if I assist your suicide, I'll inherit eighty-seven million dollars?

CAROLYN: Plus the house.

VERONIKA: Eighty-seven million plus the house.

CAROLYN: All verifiable. I'll show you my entire portfolio, if necessary.

VERONIKA: (*Weighing it in her mouth:*) Eighty-seven *million* dollars . . .

CAROLYN: But actually that's not what I'm trying to tell you. What I'm really trying to tell you is if I'm not dead by the end of your shift, I'm going to have to make another call to Martin.

(*Pause.*)

VERONIKA: Wow, I was so wrong. You're not Vader. You're Satan.

CAROLYN: Oh come on. You're missing your own point. You asked me to consider the possibility that I'm having an impact on your life, right? That I may be of some *use* to you. Well, now I'm asking you to consider the possibility—*the very real and immediate possibility*—that I may be of more use to you dead.

ENGAGEMENT RULES

by Rich Orloff

CHARACTERS: PHIL and **ROSE**, seventies

CIRCUMSTANCE: In Phil and Rose's San Diego apartment. Phil reads the newspaper as Rose enters with flowers.

PHIL: You know, I really don't believe in the death penalty, but every time I read about Congress, I'm willing to make exceptions.

ROSE: Smell these flowers. Isn't it wonderful flowers exist? Don't they just fill you with joy?

PHIL: This is a trick question, isn't it?

ROSE: What makes you say that?

PHIL: Fifty-three years of marriage.

ROSE: When you look at these flowers, don't you think there might be a higher power?

PHIL: No, I look at these flowers, and I think there'll be a line on my credit card statement: flowers.

ROSE: Do you know how many years it's been since you've been inside a church?

PHIL: I figure I don't need to keep track because God and my wife are doing it for me.

ROSE: Just once.

PHIL: Rose, ever since you started going back to church—

ROSE: Once. If you don't like it, I won't ask again.

PHIL: That's what you said before our first kid, and we ended up with three.

ROSE: Will going once kill you?

PHIL: Yep. The minister will start a sermon, I'll attack him, and he'll kill me in self-defense.

ROSE: Phil, what if there is a God?

PHIL: He hasn't made today's paper, that's for sure.

ROSE: I'd like your company.

PHIL: No you wouldn't. You'd like the company of the imaginary man who's like me in every way except that *he* likes going to church.

ROSE: It's only an hour.

PHIL: No, the service is only an hour. Then there's coffee and cookies, and all these caffeinated Christians will start shaking my hand.

ROSE: Phil—

PHIL: Rose, did I complain when you insisted we move to San Diego?

ROSE: The doctor said—

PHIL: Did I complain when you started working with Donna at San Diego Women for Equality?

ROSE: They're fighting for your rights, too.

PHIL: I don't even like half the rights I have. But okay, if it has meaning for you, fine. I'm 100% behind you. Sometimes I'm way behind you, but I'm still behind you. But this is where I draw the line. I don't believe in church, and if God were forced to sit through the average Sunday service, he wouldn't believe in it either.

ROSE: Just once. Once.

PHIL: You are the most obstinate, difficult woman I've ever met.

ROSE: It really bugs you that we're evenly matched, doesn't it?

FOOLISH FISHGIRLS AND THE PEARL

by Barbara Pease Weber

CHARACTERS: MARINA, fifties, and PEARL, twenties

CIRCUMSTANCE: These two are not what they seem at first.

MARINA: (*to* PEARL:) Listen, sweetie. CAN—YOU—UN-DER-STAND—WHAT—I'M—SAY-ING?

(PEARL *nods affirmatively.*)

Good. Take our advice. GO—BACK—TO—THE—SEA. Young sailor upstairs isn't worth it.

(PEARL *shakes her head in disagreement.*)

Now! You listen. We know! We've been where you are. Have you been listening to my tale of woe?

(PEARL *nods her head.*)

I was involved with *the Captain* for nearly thirty years! Thirty years! In the beginning, I was sure that *love would keep us together.* (*She realizes what she just said, cringes and shoots a look to* CORAL.) *Don't say it!*

CORAL: (*Smirking.*) I'm just listening. (*Beat.*) *Toe Nail.*

MARINA: (*Continuing to* PEARL:) But, when my treasure finally ran out, *the Captain* discarded me like a worn out life ring! I know I was supposed to relinquish my treasure all at once in consideration of my falling in love with a human. I admit it. *I broke the rules.* But I did it as more or less a marine insurance policy. To keep *the Captain* around. After all, I saw how things turned out for Coral and Oceana and I didn't want to end up like them. My scheme actually worked for quite a long while. I safeguarded my treasure. *The Captain* never knew where. But, it ran out eventually. And, with the way the price of gold fluctuates these days on the open market, your treasure may not even be worth as much as you think! Oh sure, you're young and beautiful and rich *now*. But, when your beauty starts to fade, and age creeps up on you like a hungry cockroach, and your sailor spends your treasure on silly boy toys, you'll curse the day you shimmied out of the ocean. So, shoo! Go back! Before it's too late. *The clock is ticking!*

HOW TO MAKE A ROPE SWING

by Shawn Fisher

CHARACTERS: ARTHUR, seventies; MICK twenties

CIRCUMSTANCE: They are packing boxes full of old school materials for disposal.

ARTHUR: You even know who that was?

MICK: Of course I know—

ARTHUR: *Who* he then?

MICK: He's—

ARTHUR: *Who* he then?! (*Beat.*) See you don't know.

MICK: I know. Everybody knows who Jackie Robinson was.

ARTHUR: If you know, then say something that isn't dumb. Go'head.

(MICK *writes "Jackie Robinson" on the chalkboard.*)

MICK: My report is on Jackie Robinson, one of the greatest men in American history—

ARTHUR: Just flappin' your gums. Trying to look smart. (*Laughs.*)

MICK: (*Still reciting.*) Jackie Robinson broke the color barrier in Major League Baseball. While all other African American ball players were relegated to the so-called Negro Leagues—

ARTHUR: Oh "relegated"? . . . You learn that in them classes of yours? Just 'cause you took two years of college—

MICK: While all other African American ball players were re-le-gat-ed . . . You can look that up, old man—

ARTHUR: Oh I know what it means.

MICK: . . . to the Negro Leagues, Jackie was able to smash down the walls that separated men by color—

ARTHUR: Oh you on a first-name basis even, callin' him Jackie. I see. "Smash down the walls?" Please. He didn't smash nothin'. Just 'cause he was the first, don't mean he *broke* the color barrier. He did no breakin'. Now Larry Doby . . . He did some breakin'. (*Pause, no response.*) You don't know who Larry Doby is? (*He changes the writing to "Larry Doby."*) Now start talking. (*Laughs.*)

MICK: (*Pauses.*) So what! I don't know who Larry Doby was.

ARTHUR: Is . . . You don't know who he *is*. He ain't dead yet. Don't go killin' him off before his time. Now who he is, is the second one to play in the Major Leagues. But he was the first one to break, or should I say, smash the color barrier.

MICK: Not Robinson?

ARTHUR: Nope.

MICK: Wasn't he first?

ARTHUR: Yup.

MICK: Wasn't he black?

ARTHUR: Come on now!

MICK: Huh. He did play baseball, right?

ARTHUR: Awww, you are getting dumber with every word you say. It's like with each syllable that you breathe out, you leak a couple IQ points. (*Beat.*) Yeah, he played ball, and he was first, and he was black. (*Pause.*) He was the "right kind" of black. The "right kind of negro" they said. See, he been to college. And he talked . . . he talked like your folk.

MICK: My folk? Shoot. My folk farmed oysters down on the bay. They didn't sound like they been to college. They sound like they got socked in the mouth and come up missing a few teeth. Like my Aunt Margie . . . She looked just like a fat sweaty little sunburned jack-o-lantern. (*Pause.*) So you're saying he wasn't "black" black.

ARTHUR: Oh don't go black-blacking on me! You don't know a damn thing about black-black. Let me tell you something. Everybody knows that the greatest ball club of all time was the 1935 Pittsburgh Crawfords of the Negro Leagues. Right? Everybody with half a brain knows that.

MICK: I didn't know that.

ARTHUR: My point exactly. They were called the "Yankees of Black Baseball," which was a generous compliment to the Yankees of white baseball. Oscar Charleston, Cool Papa Bell, Ted "Double Duty" Radcliffe . . . I's just five years old but I knew every one of 'em. But see, that didn't matter, because they weren't allowed to play the white Yankees. They didn't get to play in the real World Series. (*Pause.*) That's where the other brother comes in, round 'bout (*Beat.*) thirteen years later.

MICK: Larry Doby.

ARTHUR: La-rry Do-by! That's right! He did the breakin'. Weren't no question when he did it neither. Fourth game of the '48 Series. That's the World Series. The *white* one. Indians-Braves. Doby step up, people calling him coon, jackamammy, and few names I won't repeat. They scared of the *black boogie-man*, see. Every time he step up half the place'd boo and hiss and the rest'd go out for a hotdog. I'll tell you what, he made them hotdog vendors rich just by stepping up to the plate! (*Laughs.*) But then . . . (*Takes an old spanking paddle out of a box and mimes a batter.*) . . .with one swing, one mighty swing, they's choking on them dogs. CRACK! (*Swings, whistles, and gestures the path of a baseball.*) Four hundred, four fifty, maybe even five hundred feet of screaming baseball later and he changes some minds! From then on, people were still scared of him. But it wasn't the black boogieman no more. Nah. Now they were scared of that mighty *mighty* swing!

LADY-LIKE

by Laura Shamas

CHARACTERS: ELEANOR, late sixties; SARAH, early fifties

CIRCUMSTANCE: Year: about 1825, Plas Newydd, Wales. Eleanor and Sarah enjoy a highly unconventional relationship for that time and place. In this scene, they decide to make a slow round of their garden.

SARAH: Eleanor, I have thought for some time that we might sit for a portrait.

ELEANOR: Sarah, we can't afford to.

SARAH: It will be a symbol of our union. And we've had a volunteer. It's a woman. And a Lady at that. Lady Leighton.

ELEANOR: Will she flatter us?

SARAH: That's the point, I believe.

ELEANOR: I will sit for a half hour a day. Only!

SARAH: But that's nothing.

ELEANOR: She must take it or find another winsome pair to paint.

SARAH: An hour a day would be better.

ELEANOR: Well—

SARAH: I'll notify her that we accept.

ELEANOR: Oh, all right, my Beloved. If it means that much to you.

(*Pushes cup away.*)

SARAH: Thank you. Is that all you're going to drink?

ELEANOR: Yes.

SARAH: Really, Eleanor. You need sustenance. As you get older, you have the appetite of a bird. Soon you'll be pecking at me.

(SARAH *clears away the tea. She exits into the kitchen. There is a pause.*)

ELEANOR: (*Momentarily lost.*) Sarah! Sarah!

SARAH: (*Pops head in.*) What is it?

ELEANOR: Where did you go?

SARAH: To the kitchen, dearest.

ELEANOR: I did not know you'd left.

SARAH I never really leave you. Did you want more breakfast?

ELEANOR: (*Disoriented.*) What? What time is it? What day?

SARAH: Morning. Are you ready for our Home Circuit? It's Wednesday.

ELEANOR: I do not remember going to bed.

SARAH: Come on. The sunshine will do you good. We'll jog and jog your memory, too. (*They stand from the table and start to make a tour of their garden. Calling offstage:*) Mary, we're going for the Home Circuit!

(SARAH *grabs a cane and gives it to* ELEANOR. ELEANOR *and* SARAH *walk slowly. They stop at each point; it is their ritual.*)

The carnations are iridescent, are they not, in this light?

ELEANOR: Lovely.

SARAH: I love the scarlet tinge that the morning light can give them. There is no color like it on earth.

ELEANOR: Indeed, it is otherworldly.

SARAH: Breathe in the lilacs.

(*They inhale.*)

ELEANOR: Intoxicating.

SARAH: What do you think of the crocuses?

ELEANOR: As lovely as spring itself. It is quite green, today.

SARAH: Which color do you prefer?

ELEANOR: The purple, most definitely.

(SARAH *pauses, then continues.*)

SARAH: The purple, really?

ELEANOR: They've always outshone the yellow. I tolerate the yellow only to highlight the purple.

SARAH: None of the purple are up yet, dearest.

(SARAH *waves her arm in front of* ELEANOR'*s eyes slowly.*)

ELEANOR: Surely they are. It is late enough—

SARAH: No. None are up.

ELEANOR: (*Angrily:*) It is the sunlight, blinding me.

SARAH: You've been hiding this, your blindness—

ELEANOR: It will come back. Some days I can see better than others.

SARAH: The doctor said the time would come for an operation. I'd better arrange it.

ELEANOR: I don't want that. Sarah. I told you.

SARAH: He says it is the only way to save an infection from spreading.

ELEANOR: I don't want a knife in my eye.

SARAH: You're as blind as a bat. We must take some action to rectify your vision before it gets beyond repair.

ELEANOR: If I'm already as blind as a bat, a knife in the eye won't help a thing.

SARAH: We must try.

ELEANOR: The doctor has so convinced you.

SARAH: It is for your own good. I'm trying to take care of you as best I can.

(*They finish rounding off the Home Circuit.*)

ELEANOR: They'll have to apply leeches. I despise leeches.

SARAH: Try and endure it, so that we may have twenty more blissful years together.

MEMORY HOUSE

by Kathleen Tolan

CHARACTERS: MAGGIE, mid-fifties; KATIA, eighteen

CIRCUMSTANCE: In Maggie's kitchen, Maggie and her daughter Katia are forced to grapple with the past as they face an uncertain future.

MAGGIE: I'm not holding myself up as an example.

KATIA: You shouldn't.

MAGGIE: I'm not. Thank god I have my baking, always a source for solace.

(MAGGIE *checks the pie in the oven, adjusts the temperature.*)

KATIA: You used to be a *dancer*.

MAGGIE: Really?

KATIA: You used to have a *company*.

MAGGIE: I did?

KATIA: You used to have a *life*.

MAGGIE: I have a life.

KATIA: You used to *dance*.

MAGGIE: I still dance.

KATIA: When I'm over at Dad's?

MAGGIE: Yes. And in my head. Much more efficient. And easier on the bod. I do apologize for having succumbed to the inevitable descent and decay, I know that it's humiliating to you, mortifying and I realize that you don't bring your friends around anymore it's mortifying to witness the descent and decay though, just a guess, I think you'll understand, in time.

KATIA: I won't.

MAGGIE: You know, not everybody figures out how to be a big shining star, most people find jobs and do work and have hobbies and occasionally weep at the wall because it feels sad, that's what people do. I hope you have a bright and shiny life but I doubt if you'll avoid a few little failures—

KATIA: I know that.

MAGGIE: A few disappointments and regrets—

KATIA: Disappointments maybe but not regrets. I hate that you have regrets.

MAGGIE: But I'd say that it would be helpful to get your applications in. Not that educated people are happier than uneducated people, I've read the surveys—

KATIA: Stop.

MAGGIE: (*Loses it, erupts:*) Fine. Fuck it. Crash and burn. Go for it. I don't give a flying fuck.

(*Silence.*)

Why are you here, anyway? Why did you come over? Why have you parked yourself in my living room? Why don't you go crash and burn at Daddy's? I have things to do.

KATIA: Oh. Sorry.

MAGGIE: You think I want to be here? You think I give a flying fuck about this fucking pie? I don't care. I don't care at all.

KATIA: Okay.

MAGGIE: I don't care if you fucking blow it, okay?

KATIA: Well why the fuck are you baking the fucking pie and going on and on and on about what a fucking revelation it is as if anybody cares, why don't you leave, why don't you go?

MAGGIE: Because this is my living room.

KATIA: And it's not mine.

MAGGIE: Yes it is.

KATIA: No it's not. I don't have a home. I don't have a place. There's no place that is home. I don't belong anywhere.

MAGGIE: You belong here. You belong with me. And with your father. And your friends. And in school. And in college. This is modern life.

KATIA: Oh, god, please, not another lecture.

MAGGIE: Modern Life. A Lecture. An essay! Just write it. Just do it. Don't think about it.

KATIA: I can't.

MAGGIE: You can.

KATIA: It isn't your business.

MAGGIE: It is my business. Then my life's work will be done and I can lie down and die.

KATIA: That is what you think.

MAGGIE: You wish.

KATIA: I know.

RACHEL HOLDS COURT

by Bara Swain

CHARACTERS: RACHEL (*sixties–seventies*): an energetic and vital single Jewish woman. She is animated, outspoken, and overly sensitive, and tends to dominate conversations. She wears a bright sweater or cardigan and chemise, diamond-studded earrings and pendant. Her lipstick is bright red. Rachel lives in Queens and commutes to NYC for work; **LENORE** (*sixties–seventies*): personable but less flamboyant. She is practical, and lacks Rachel's confidence and experience in the romance arena. She wears black liquid eyeliner and is dressed in a patterned blouse, slacks or skirt, and a chemise. She is also single and lives in Queens.

CIRCUMSTANCE: In Lenore's home in Queens, New York, feisty Rachel reveals more than she intends when she dispenses dating advice to Lenore.

(RACHEL *and* LENORE *are discovered in* LENORE's *home in the middle of a conversation.*)

LENORE: Rachel?

RACHEL: Yeah.

LENORE: I don't want to grow old alone.

RACHEL: Nobody does. (*Thoughtfully.*) Maybe you'll grow old with the accountant.

LENORE: We don't have a lot in common.

(*Silence.*)

Rachel?

RACHEL: Yeah.

LENORE: What's the difference between a lawyer and an accountant?

RACHEL: (*Hesitates.*) An accountant knows he's boring.

LENORE: (*Gloomily.*) That's the only thing Aaron and I have in common.

RACHEL: (*Gently.*) If your basic values are similar, I don't think it matters, Lenore. Sometimes it's more fun to celebrate your differences, you know?

(LENORE *doesn't answer. Silence.*)

Do you respect him?

LENORE: I don't like his sense of humor.

RACHEL: At least he *has* a sense of humor.

LENORE: "You've got a lovely pair of W-2s, Lenore." (*Rolls her eyes.*) "If I help you screw Uncle Sam, will you screw me?"

(*Shaking head.*) If he'd just shut up for a minute, I think I'd feel more romantic, more—you know—inclined to have a sexual relationship with him. Only half the things that come out of Aaron's mouth are too crude and too . . . intimate for me.

RACHEL: Why wouldn't you want intimacy?

LENORE: It's too much information! I don't want to know so many details. And then he calls me every single night, emails three times a day, calls me again if I don't answer an email, and—

RACHEL: —Whoa, whoa. Let me get this straight. Aaron is an attentive, loving man with a good job, a sense of humor, and a healthy sexual appetite, who wants to share the details of his life with you. And you're what—complaining?

(LENORE *picks up a sheet of paper off the table and reads.*)

LENORE: "Dear Lenore. Now here's a new one for the age of laptops. I can actually begin writing this email while sitting on the toilet . . . (*She hesitates.*) . . . pooing. Sometimes it gets difficult because I have to hold my penis while either holding the computer or typing with one hand, but it works. (*Grimacing.*) I know we are very different this way, and you really did not need to know this information. Sleep well, my Princess. Huge hugs and deep long kisses, you gorgeous, sexy woman of mine. Love, Aaron"

(*Silence.*)

RACHEL: You really want my advice?

(LENORE *nods.*)

Then here's my advice. Grow up, Lenore. None of us are perfect. And the older we get, the more flawed we are. So we talk too much and we mix up metaphors. Big deal! We're afraid of jaywalking but we smoke two packs a day. So what? We sing during commercials and we sleep during *Madame Butterfly*. Who cares! I think it's time for you to look at the big picture—the BIG PICTURE, dear—and either start lowering your expectations . . . or stop living!

(LENORE *is angry and hurt. She tries to maintain a steady voice.*)

LENORE: My expectations or my standards, Rachel? I didn't sleep with Dr. Bukberg's entire patient roster! Oh, wait a second. You're not a slut. You're overly sensitive!

RACHEL: Once you've calmed down, I expect an apology, Lenore. But until then . . .

LENORE: Don't treat me like a child. You're not my mother!

(RACHEL *rises from her chair and crosses to exit.* LENORE *calls out after her.*)

Thank God you never had any children. AND I WANT MY SWEATER BACK, RACHEL!

RACHEL: (*Quietly.*) I'll get it dry-cleaned and return it to you as soon as—

LENORE: NOW!

> (LENORE *unbuttons the rest of her blouse. She removes it.*)

> Here. Here's your dead mother's blouse. Wear it in good health. Now, I'd like the sweater.

RACHEL: But . . .

LENORE: Since when do you need to be asked twice to remove your clothing, Rachel.

(RACHEL *turns her back to* LENORE. *She hesitates. Slowly and carefully* RACHEL *pulls the sweater over her head. Pause. She turns to* LENORE, *shielding her chest with her hands. They stare at each other. Slowly,* RACHEL *lowers her hands. Visible—above her chemise—are electrodes and connecting wires down to her pocket.* SHE *is wearing a halter monitor. Silence. The only movement is* RACHEL's *quivering chin. Then* RACHEL's *face contorts in anguish. The only sound is her soft weeping.* RACHEL *holds* LENORE's *gaze. As the lights fade,* LENORE *crosses towards her friend.*)

RAINBOW SPRINKLES

by Stacey Lane

CHARACTERS: MIRANDA GILES-HAMPTON, fifty-six; RAINBOW SPRINKLES, seventy-three

CIRCUMSTANCE: An ornate, classy office of Miranda, an executive lawyer in a well-known firm. She is interviewing a clown, Rainbow Sprinkles, for a birthday party.

MIRANDA: Please explain to me what your general birthday party clown act consists of.

SPRINKLES: Well, as I greet the children, as they arrive, I tell them jokes and—

MIRANDA: What kind of jokes?

SPRINKLES: Oh you know, kid jokes, like—

MIRANDA: As I am sure you are aware, Mr. Noman, humor is a very sensitive topic nowadays. What may be funny to one individual, may be quite offensive to another. To joke is to poke fun at something or someone and well, Mr. Noman, we don't want to hurt anyone's feelings.

SPRINKLES: My jokes are just children's jokes, to make them laugh and smile. I assure you, ma'am, that my jokes will not offend anyone.

MIRANDA: Mr. Noman, you never can know for certain what will offend people these days and I for one am simply not willing to take that risk at my grandson's party. I think that it would just make my heart feel much more at ease, if we just cancelled the joke portion of the afternoon. I am sure you understand.

SPRINKLES: Ma'am, I don't see how—

MIRANDA: Well, I am glad that that is settled. Now, let's see. What else does your clown act consist of?

SPRINKLES: Well, typically after we eat the cake and open the presents, I paint faces.

MIRANDA: Hhhhmmm . . . I see. And what exactly do you paint on faces?

SPRINKLES: Oh, whatever the kid wants.

MIRANDA: Whatever the kid wants! Mr. Noman, I think you give children a tad too much credit. What if the child wants a pentagram or a swastika on his or her face? Or what if he or she wants a cross and that offends the Jewish child at the party or the Jewish child wants a Star of David and that offends the Christian child?

SPRINKLES: Kids usually ask for balloons, smiley faces, flowers, hearts, things like that.

MIRANDA: Hearts! Do you think that little ten-year-old girls at my grandson's party need to have hearts on their faces, as if they are just begging for a romantic relationship at such a young and impressionable age?

SPRINKLES: I am sure that is not what they mean by—

MIRANDA: Not to mention, the chance of a child having an allergic reaction to the makeup you put on him or her.

SPRINKLES: I use high quality makeup and have never had a problem before—

MIRANDA: Furthermore, it's not quite sanitary, using the same makeup on each child.

SPRINKLES: I clean the brush between each use.

MIRANDA: With what?

SPRINKLES: Water.

MIRANDA: Make it some sort of non-scented hypoallergenic sanitizer and I suppose that should appease most of the mothers. I will tell you what I will do for you, Mr. Noman. You can draw me some basic images that you might want to paint and I will approve the politically correct ones.

SPRINKLES: Well, I suppose that maybe—

MIRANDA: On second thought, some of your face paintings might come out nicer than others and then the children may not feel like equals. The parents may feel that you are playing favorites. It would probably be in the best interest of all involved if we just cut the face painting from our little party lineup.

SPRINKLES: But, ma'am, I—

MIRANDA: Now, Mr. Noman, you seem to be a reasonable gentleman and I am sure you understand my situation as a legal guardian and my desire to take all precautions to ensure that my grandson has the best birthday party he or anyone else on the block has ever had. I am glad that that matter is settled. Now, what else do you have on your agenda?

SPRINKLES: Well, after the kids have had a chance to play on their own a little, I usually sit them down for the big event, my magic show. I must say that I am quite proud of it. It is one of the best that I have ever seen.

MIRANDA: Do you use a rabbit?

SPRINKLES: Actually, yes, I do. Mr. Hoppity. He has been with me for five years now.

MIRANDA: Cut the rabbit. The animal rights activists would have a field day with that one.

THE SECRET ORDER

by Robert Clyman

CHARACTERS: **ROBERT BROCK**, fifties, immunologist and director of Hill-Matheson. A charismatic man of great intelligence and ambition. **SAUL ROTH**, sixty-seven, chief of toxicology at Hill-Matheson. Plays at being the amiable philosopher but is in fact a very political animal.

CIRCUMSTANCE: Brock and Roth are rivals for power. Robert Brock, a previous runner-up for the Nobel in his younger days, was brought in a year ago as the new director to restore the prestigious Hill-Matheson Institute for Cancer Research to its former glory. During his brief tenure, he has already alienated many department chiefs. His most powerful adversary is Saul Roth, the chief of Toxicology, whose days of original research are well behind him, and whom Brock regards as emblematic of Hill-Matheson's diminishing, moribund stature.

(*Lights up on* BROCK's *office, as* BROCK *ushers* ROTH *in.*)

BROCK: Saul, come in and sit. Coffee?

ROTH: Please.

BROCK: With a little milk. You see? I remember.

ROTH: Will you let me say something? Right here, right now, I insist.

(*Slight beat.*)

Bravo. To a successful first year at the helm. Some directors, when they get here, they do a little this, a little that . . . but not you.

BROCK: There isn't time.

ROTH: You said, "The hell with Toxicology. Chemo can go fly a kite. Fuck anyone but me and mine." Which is how it should be . . . to a point. And the point is this. I heard a rumor about your Dr. Shumway . . . according to which, you asked the board to put certain monies at his disposal.

BROCK: I'm not sure why you call it a rumor.

ROTH: My Uncle Milt . . . a very wealthy man . . . used to say, "Never get too close to one idea." He was Sephardic . . . came over in the Diaspora on a camel . . .

BROCK: Saul . . . please. This is a copy of my new budget.

ROTH: (*As he reads.*) You don't imagine the board'll approve this arrogant . . . ?

BROCK: I can assure you they agonized before doing just that ten minutes ago.

(*Beat.*)

I understand your disappointment, Saul. Really, I do. So I wouldn't think of you as disloyal, if you were to consider other offers that might come along.

ROTH: (*Genuinely stunned.*) I'm sixty-seven years old. My wife and I are very . . . comfortable here.

BROCK: I seem to remember you've got a daughter living in Dallas, husband works for Raytheon? Maybe you could find something closer . . . get to see more of your grandchildren.

ROTH: You know, now that I'm looking more closely, did I say I couldn't live with these? A man can't get to be sixty-seven, he doesn't see flexible as a virtue.

BROCK: The thing is, Saul, it isn't just money for your projects. I'm cutting salaries, too.

ROTH: Well, then . . . I don't see the problem. My wife, she likes to shop. Thirty-two years, I've told her what can you buy at Bloomingdale's that Macy's hasn't got? So, exactly how much were you thinking?

BROCK: I really don't want to insult you.

ROTH: Please . . . insult me.

BROCK: The fact is, I could get three post-docs with the money I'm paying you.

ROTH: Three more years, Bob, I'm seventy. That's when a man is supposed to be old. I'll lie on the beach in Miami . . . go hear Eydie Gorme . . . in the meantime, all I need is an office with my name on the door. A place to go each morning, I can put on a suit.

BROCK: Saul, I'm really not the bastard you think I am. If you would still like to stay / on . . .

ROTH: Ask anyone, Bob, I never used the word "bastard."

BROCK: . . . But about your own office, I don't see how. You know the problems with space here.

ROTH: I guess I didn't make myself clear. The money, I already told you . . . make me an offer, the answer is yes. But at sixty-seven, without my own office . . . I shouldn't have to explain / this to . . .

BROCK: Saul, it isn't just you. I talked with Howard this morning. I'm merging him and Chemo as of / the eighth.

ROTH: All due respect, Bob, Howard's a kid.

(*Holding up the list of projects.*)

These I can swallow. The office, though, I have to insist.

BROCK: No, Saul, you don't get to insist. Not anymore.

(*Beat.*)

So, what do you think?

ROTH: What do I think? Fuck you, is what I think. I've had an office for thirty-three years . . . since the day I got here from Hopkins.

BROCK: It's in the order of things, Saul . . . I'm sorry.

ROTH: I've been here through four different directors. At some point, every one of them needed my support . . . when that day comes for you . . .

BROCK: You wanted to meet, so we're meeting. I could've just sent you a memo.

SOUTHERN FRIED FUNERAL

by Osborne and Eppler

CHARACTER: UNCLE DUB, fifties–sixties; **DOROTHY**, fifties–sixties

CIRCUMSTANCE: Feigning kindness, Uncle Dub is taking Dorothy's house. Just back from a funeral, they chat politely in Dorothy's soon-to-be-lost home.

UNCLE DUB: Dorothy, it was a wonderful service. I know Dewey would have enjoyed it immensely if he hadn't been the guest of honor.

DOROTHY: Yes, Dub. It was nice. Is there something you needed?

UNCLE DUB: I just wanted to check on you and see how you were doing.

DOROTHY: Fine, I guess. Just kind of numb. And I want to thank you for giving me a distraction. I needed something to take my mind off Dewey passing. I just didn't know it was going to come in the form of an eviction notice.

UNCLE DUB: Well, I thought it was downright honorable giving you thirty days' notice.

DOROTHY: Well, I don't want to look a gift horse in the mouth, but thirty days ain't a real long time. Just for my own edification, why do you have want this old house?

UNCLE DUB: I thought I explained that I don't want the house. Just the land. You are more than welcome to move the house to a location of your choosing.

DOROTHY: Now you're just splitting hairs. Okay then, why do you want the land? What are you going to do with it? It's been thirty years since you've done anything with the land next door. Why all of a sudden do you care? You're up to something, Dub Frye. Now tell me what it is.

UNCLE DUB: Well, I wanted to surprise you, but I reckon you're just not gonna let that happen. Okay then, where we stand now, there will be a brand new Big Value Hardware and Garden Center.

DOROTHY: I beg your pardon.

UNCLE DUB: That's right. It's gonna be one of the largest in the southeast.

DOROTHY: When did this happen? Have you just been sittin' around waiting for your brother to die so you could get your hands on this land?

UNCLE DUB: No ma'am. I was gonna cut him in on it. But he died before I could tell him.

DOROTHY: Dub Frye, I have known you for almost forty years and the nicest thing I can say about you is that you always pick up the cats out of the road after you run them over. You have always been a snake in the grass and now you're showing your true colors.

UNCLE DUB: Is it wrong for a man to get ahead in this world?

DOROTHY: It is if you have to step on folks' heads on your way up. Dewey never had to step on anybody to get where he was. And he may not have had the political aspirations that you did, but by God he was a good, decent, honest man. That's why more than half the town showed up today to send him to his glory. Just think about this, Dub Frye, how many folks do you think will show up for your service when you go? I'll tell you how many. One: the preacher and that's only 'cause he's getting paid to be there.

UNCLE DUB: I thought we could be civil about this. But it's a done deal. I'm taking the land and that's it.

DOROTHY: Oh no. You're takin' the house, too. You're gonna have to deal with it. I don't have the money nor the inclination to move this house all over tarnation and back. You want it? You can have it! Here's what you can take from me . . . the doorjamb where all the kids had their height measured every year. All the pictures going up the staircase. The dress I was wearing when Dewey and I went on our first date. Then there's the crutches from Harlene broke her leg at the skatin' rink and Sammy Jo's four hundred debate trophies and Dewdrop's Tammy Wynette CD collection and all the games in the game closet including the Scrabble game that Harlene took all the S's out of so Sammy Jo couldn't spell her name. And everything else in my life. Because if you take this house, that's what you're taking. Not just a house, not just a piece of land, but my life. So take it all! You slimy son of a—.

SPOOK

by Alan Bowne

CHARACTERS: LOLLY, fifty; ELEANOR, mid-forties

CIRCUMSTANCE: In a windswept house on the coast of Maine, two single women—one who has had success in romance, one who has not—discuss the presence of a handsome and highly sensual ghost in their home.

LOLLY: Sensitive! Well, I'm not. God knows, I've always been what they call in California a "skag." For years I fought against it, but finally a woman can never rise above her body-type, can she? Men slot you into a category, and there you stay, caught for all time in anatomical amber. So naturally I was surprised when he passed you over and settled on plain old me. Though between a middle-aged frump and an aging alcoholic—

ELEANOR: Yes, it was obviously *slim pickings* for the poor thing, but do get to the point, Lolly.

LOLLY: The point?

ELEANOR: The *dirty* part.

LOLLY: The point, Eleanor, is that he isn't an ordinary man. Not like men living today.

ELEANOR: Oh, we've all had fantasies of a swashbuckling lover out of *Anthony Adverse*.

LOLLY: He's *not* a creation of Hollywood. Neither is he bound by conventions or passing standards. He's free. He's large.

ELEANOR: (*Ironic; glancing pointedly at easel.*) Whopping!

LOLLY: Oh, I don't say he isn't lusty. It was part of life, and it burns in him still. An unappeasable hunger. (*Pausing by easel.*) That's what I was trying to catch here. It's not that he's intent on achieving some wretched penile blurt. He's not a *modern* man, with lusts the size of his stunted horizons.

ELEANOR: Good god, that's prose out of a dollar-fifty gothic!

LOLLY: He's a force of nature! Open, unashamed, irresistible. I suppose that's essentially why he chose me.

ELEANOR: I beg your pardon?

LOLLY: He required a kind of purity.

ELEANOR: Sweet of you to say it.

LOLLY: Oh, I don't mean sexual purity. I mean a purity in the nerves. Clear, trusting, unbruised nerves. He *didn't* want to possess a paranoid person.

ELEANOR: So you admit it. You're possessed.

LOLLY: Isn't a woman always? By the simple weight of a man, the smell of him?

ELEANOR: You *smell* him?

LOLLY: Of course. Pretty rank, actually. But then everything about him is intense.

ELEANOR: Yes, men do have characteristic body odors. What's *his* like?

LOLLY: Beans.

ELEANOR: *Beans?*

LOLLY: Baked beans.

ELEANOR: How appropriate, as Boston's so close. So throughout your—congress—he's more or less human? Substantial. Glandular.

LOLLY: Smooth. Juicy. On the mechanical level. Yes.

ELEANOR: Well, that's the level I'm interested in.

LOLLY: Yes, I was always interested in the mechanics, too, at first. But aren't we always? Initially we want the physical thrill, don't we? And then that's not enough and we want something else, we're not sure what. And it's precisely there, I take it, that material men don't deliver.

IAN AND CAROL SCENE FROM

THE HERD

by Rory Kinnear

CHARACTERS: CAROL, fifties, sixties; IAN, fifties, sixties

CIRCUMSTANCE: In Carol's home, it's the twenty-first birthday party of Ian and Carol's severely disabled son.

CAROL: What are you doing here?

IAN: I wanted to see Andy. On his birthday.

CAROL: Why didn't you call?

(*A moment.*)

IAN: I didn't think you'd let me come.

CAROL: But you came anyway.

IAN: Yes.

CAROL: For God's sake . . . Just get some ice.

(IAN *goes to the freezer and gets out the ice tray.*)

IAN: Do you have a tea towel?

CAROL: Third drawer down.

(IAN *takes out a tea towel, puts some ice in it and holds it to his lip.*)

IAN: How is he?

CAROL: Perhaps you might explain why you're here before we start on the medical review.

IAN: Carol, this wasn't a spur of the moment thing.

CAROL: Well thanks for letting us know.

(*A moment.*)

IAN: It's his twenty-first birthday.

CAROL: I know.

IAN: It was important for me to see him.

CAROL: Really.

IAN: Carol. This isn't totally comfortable for me either.

(*Silence.*)

I don't know what to say.

CAROL: Oh say something, for Christ's sake. If you've been thinking about it so long.

IAN: I can't say everything I need to can I?

CAROL: Why not?

IAN: Because it would take a while wouldn't it?

CAROL: It would take until the end of time.

(*A moment.*)

IAN: If you honestly can't bear the thought of me seeing him then I'll go.

CAROL: That's right, walk out when things get difficult. That makes a change.

IAN: I have not come here to argue with you. I came here to see Andy. I don't want to start arguing with you again . . .

CAROL: Oh thank you, Gandhi.

IAN: But if you can't see a way that that could happen then I will leave.

CAROL: Oh yes, very good. The martyr returns to his wife saying "I did all I could."

IAN: Fine, Carol. Will you give him this?

CAROL: You coward. Fucking fight.

(*A moment.*)

IAN: What?

CAROL: Fucking fight to see him you fucking coward.

(*Silence.*)

Why do you want to see him Ian? Why today, why now?

IAN: I've told you. Because it's his birthday.

CAROL: And?

IAN: And what?

CAROL: Why this birthday? What was wrong with the others?

IAN: I am aware I've not been there for him of late . . .

CAROL: Right.

IAN: . . . and that it has been difficult . . .

CAROL: Difficult?

IAN: . . . but I want to see my son.

CAROL: So it's the guilt you can't live with, not Andy you can't live without.

IAN: No, it's not just . . . it's not guilt.

CAROL: And did you honestly expect . . . did you really think that by coming here . . . did you actually believe that by just turning up, unannounced, uninvited, with a fucking present, that we would fall to our knees and say "Oh thank you, oh praise the Lord He is risen, alle- fucking-luia"? Did you?

IAN: Of course I . . .

CAROL: Because actually Ian I have done this by myself for the last twenty years. Throughout. By myself. You not showing your face for the last five years, it hasn't actually made a blind fucking difference to my life.

IAN: And you don't think that might have had anything to do with it?

CAROL: What?

IAN: Doesn't matter.

(*A moment.*)

CAROL: No, what do you mean by that?

IAN: It doesn't matter. Please.

(*Silence.*)

CAROL: Are you dying?

IAN: Dying?

CAROL: Well it's too late for a midlife crisis, you've done that already. Is it Sylvie? Have you split up with her?

IAN: No.

CAROL: Has she been pressuring you?

IAN: This is nothing to do with Sylvie. Or with Paul.

CAROL: It must be somehow. This *was* your family. They *are* your family. There must be parallels somewhere.

IAN: This isn't fair.

CAROL: They must feel like they're waiting for that axe to fall too, no? If things get a bit tricky. Sorry, how is it not fair?

IAN: You know that's not how things were. Or are.

CAROL: No I don't know Ian. I don't fucking know at all.

(*They are silent.*)

IAN: Life was not easy. Eventually. Between the two of us. Was it?

CAROL: No it was fucking hard. And for some of us it's got even harder.

IAN: For both of us.

(*A moment.*)

CAROL: I honestly can't . . . I understood when you left us, I understood you couldn't cope. I understood when you met Sylvie, when you had Paul. But not to see him for five years. And then to come here, on his birthday, seeking some sort of absolution from him . . . that, Ian, I can't even begin to understand.

IAN: I have been in contact with him. I do call him. I write.

CAROL: Yes, he's a voracious reader. And he just loves to chat . . .

IAN: Fine, I didn't see him because it got too much for me. Is that what you want to hear? I've felt like a cunt for years and now I'm sick of feeling like a cunt.

HOME FRONT

by Greg Owens

CHARACTERS: JO, fifty; DARWIN, fifty-four

CIRCUMSTANCE: A guest has come to stay in Jo and Darwin's home, causing rifts in their relationship to surface. Scene opens with Jo in the kitchen. She pours herself a cup of coffee.

(DARWIN *enters.*)

JO: How'd you sleep?

DARWIN: I didn't sleep, Jo. I stood guard outside her room all night.

JO: Oh.

DARWIN: We have to talk.

JO: I know what you're going to say.

DARWIN: She goes.

JO: Darwin—

DARWIN: No. Listen to me. I told you that girl was dangerous.

JO: I don't think Lucy meant to threaten us.

DARWIN: She came only inches from stabbing that knife into your hand.

JO: Lucy wasn't trying to hurt me. She was simply acting out. Like a child. That's what she is, Darwin. A scared, helpless child.

DARWIN: I'm calling Lincoln this morning. He said he wanted us to call if it seemed like there was anything wrong with her.

JO: Well, if you're so set on calling him, then why haven't you done it already? Since when do you need my approval on anything?

DARWIN: We've got to put up a united front. I can't bring him in here until I know what you're going to say when he comes.

JO: So, it's not that you care about my feelings, you just don't trust me.

DARWIN: Feelings have nothing to do with this.

JO: Of course not. Why should this be any different?

DARWIN: Can we please not get into all that right now?

JO: You'd better get ready. You're going to be late for your ball game.

DARWIN: I'm not going to the game.

JO: But you promised Ronnie. He'll be disappointed.

DARWIN: He'll just have to deal with that. I'm not leaving you alone in the house with that mad woman.

JO: I'm not afraid.

DARWIN: Well maybe that's because you don't have enough sense to be afraid.

JO: Don't talk to me like that.

DARWIN: I will talk to you exactly like that. I know why you're doing this, Jo.

JO: If you call him, he'll take her away.

DARWIN: Honey, you're not being rational.

JO: Why am I doing this?

(DARWIN *doesn't answer.*)

Tell me. I want to hear what you think you know about me.

DARWIN: She's not ours. We have one child. One. And that's it. That was our choice. We can't change that now.

JO: No, Darwin. That wasn't our choice. It was yours.

DARWIN: Fine. You can blame me for that 'til the end of our lives if you want.

JO: I will.

(*She turns away from him.*)

DARWIN: Josephine, can't you see that if I'm only thinking about you and Ronnie? If anything happened to you—

JO: If anything happened to us, you'd go right along as always. You'd drive to work in the morning and come home at night and read your paper. Nothing would change. It wouldn't affect you in the least.

DARWIN: That isn't true. How can you think that?

JO: You've been a ghost in this house for twenty years. You pass right through me and I can't even feel you.

THE GREAT MAN

by Charlie Schulman

CHARACTERS: The GREAT MAN, sixties+, vigorous, handsome, brilliant, alternately streetwise and erudite; the BIOGRAPHER, forties–fifties

CIRCUMSTANCE: In the Great Man's study in Maine, the Biographer is sent to convince his literary hero—the reclusive, cantankerous "Great Man"—to let him write his biography. Over time, the Biographer's sycophantic view of the great author sours, as he delves further into the great man's life and begins to contemplate the human wreckage that lies in the wake of "greatness." The Great Man and The Biographer sit facing each other.

GREAT MAN: You know I've been aware of you for a long time. Not specifically you, but the idea of you.

BIOGRAPHER: Then I hope I can live up to your expectations.

GREAT MAN: Me too. We'll see . . . I've actually written you several letters and various postcards. Mementos from my life. Souvenirs so to speak.

BIOGRAPHER: I'd love to see them.

GREAT MAN: I'm sure you would. Yes, I've always kept you near and dear to me. I knew from the time I was a young man that some day I would have a biographer. That eventually, if I didn't die an untimely death, I would meet with him and have this very discussion we're having now.

BIOGRAPHER: Then you're at an advantage because you've already thought this through.

GREAT MAN: Yes, I've had this and other discussions with you in my mind.

BIOGRAPHER: Then I hope you won't mind having them again for my benefit.

GREAT MAN: Not at all. We've discussed literature and politics. I've defended my ideas. My actions. My life. Over time I've even created something of a lasting bond with you. To be honest, it's a bond that has lasted as long as any I've ever known.

BIOGRAPHER: So you've created a fictional character in your mind's eye.

GREAT MAN: Yes, something like that.

BIOGRAPHER: The character of your biographer.

GREAT MAN: Yes.

BIOGRAPHER: And you have created a long-standing friendship with this person?

GREAT MAN: In a manner of speaking.

BIOGRAPHER: And now fiction meets reality.

GREAT MAN: Exactly.

BIOGRAPHER: And you're worried.

GREAT MAN: Yes, but I'm also eager to find out how it all works out in the end.

BIOGRAPHER: And how do you suspect it will end?

GREAT MAN: Eventually I fall out with everyone, but I hate the idea of ruining a beautiful relationship.

BIOGRAPHER: But you always knew that one day you would meet this biographer.

GREAT MAN: Yes, I suppose I did.

BIOGRAPHER: And you knew that he couldn't be the one in your mind's eye. He would actually be a real person.

GREAT MAN: Understanding and experiencing are two very different things.

BIOGRAPHER: You hope we will see eye to eye.

GREAT MAN: Naturally.

BIOGRAPHER: And you're afraid that we won't?

GREAT MAN: Nobody wants to be misunderstood—especially by his biographer. Don't get me wrong. You seem like a nice enough fellow. All writers seem nice enough . . . until you get to know them. As a writer of fiction I don't want to lose control of my own story.

BIOGRAPHER: You've read my biography of Gerhard Black?

GREAT MAN: Gerhard was brilliant, magnetic, and completely unpredictable. Your biography was fair and well researched. Except for a few minor details you seem to have gotten Gerhard right.

BIOGRAPHER: Thank you. I tried.

GREAT MAN: But biography has its limitations. I find it often gives us far greater insight into the biographer than it does his subject. I appreciate how far you traveled to get here. I very much wanted to meet with you, but I'm feeling rather tired.

BIOGRAPHER: I can come back later in the afternoon.

GREAT MAN: No, that won't be necessary. You're a fine writer. If I ever were to have a biographer I would be damn lucky if he turned out to be you.

BIOGRAPHER: I don't understand.

GREAT MAN: Contrary to what my agent or anyone else might think—I'm not dead yet and I don't intend to die any time soon. I'm still writing. Still fucking. Still making mischief and if anyone is going to be my biographer it better damn well be me. Our discussion has only further confirmed my desire to write my memoir.

BIOGRAPHER: But I thought we had an agreement.

GREAT MAN: You've talked me out of it. My assistant, Nick, can give you directions to the thruway.

THE PENETRATION PLAY

by Winter Miller

CHARACTER: MAGGIE, mid-fifties; **RAIN**, mid-twenties

CIRCUMSTANCE: Maggie's home, late night. Rain is in love with Ashley, Maggie's daughter. Ash is uncertain what she wants. Might Maggie be interested?

RAIN: I'm sorry I got you up, I—

MAGGIE: Not to worry, I was up. My friend Ellie turned me on to this mystery writer and I can't put the book down. She has a series; after the first I went out and bought all six. This time of year I devour books. There's nothing left to do in the garden, it's too hot to cook, and at night, what the hell else is there to do anyway? We rent a movie, Bill snores through it. Do you read mysteries?

RAIN: Not really. Not since Nancy Drew though I liked her.

MAGGIE: Ashley loved Nancy Drew! MY mother bought her the whole set one year—I remember they were all pink! Forty pink bindings. I know it's trite, but reading is an escape. I don't pick up the phone, I let the machine get it. Her sister and I swap books all the time, and when Ashley was in high school, she was a reader. I don't think she ever reads now . . . .

RAIN: She does some . . .

MAGGIE: Maybe she discusses them with you, but she never mentions any books and if I ask her about a best-seller most of the time she hasn't even heard of it. I don't know what she does with her free time.

RAIN: I guess it's mostly magazines . . .

MAGGIE: It's because she's out 'til all hours. She goes out an inordinate amount.

RAIN: Not that much—

MAGGIE: She's never there if I call at night. And she won't answer in the morning. The only place to reach her is at work. I don't know why I'm complaining to you. I'm sure you keep in touch with your mother.

RAIN: It depends, phases I guess—

MAGGIE: Let me get you something to drink. How about some sherry?

RAIN: I'm not sure I like sherry.

MAGGIE: I love sherry, it's one of those things that warms your entire body instantly. I can only drink it at night in this weather. How about a glass of wine, some ice cream?

RAIN: A glass of wine would be nice. I think we polished off the ice cream earlier.

MAGGIE: There's a pint of Ben & Jerry's I just saw in there.

RAIN: We decimated it, there's maybe a bite left.

MAGGIE: Oh. Well, I have an Oregonian Pinot opened, do you drink red?

RAIN: That'd be great. I feel bad I'm keeping you up?

MAGGIE: I'm gonna have a glass with you.

RAIN: Even better.

MAGGIE: Can't let you drink alone. That's Bill's job. Listen to me, I'm a bitter old hag. At least I still have my teeth.

(MAGGIE *sets down two glasses and a bottle of wine.*)

RAIN: Did you and Bill have a wild night?

MAGGIE: Always. Bill's sound asleep. He's been passed out for hours.

(*She exits to the kitchen.*)

(*Offstage, singing.*) "Que sera, sera, whatever will be, will be . . . "

Do you like cheese? He has eight cocktails before dinner with the neighbors and he's out like a light. Whoop-de-doo!

Nothing wakes him up, I have fantasies about hiring someone to drive a Mack truck through the front porch just to
see if he'd stir. I don't think he'd wake up. (*Singing.*) "The
future's not ours to see . . . que sera, sera."

RAIN: You have a nice voice.

(MAGGIE *enters with a very elaborate cheese plate.*)

MAGGIE: Not at all. I thought you might want to nibble. (*Realizing.*)
I apologize, I'm in my nightgown, pardon me for not
throwing on a robe.

RAIN: Not at all. (*Referring to the cheese.*) This is great.

MAGGIE: Ashley would be mortified.

RAIN: I love lilies, it's a pretty gown. I can't wear them—they
end up around my neck in the morning.

MAGGIE: Not that Bill would ever notice, he's too busy checking
his eyelids for holes. Careful who you end up with, that's
my advice. The prince may look charming, but chances
are, he snores, he stinks, and he's off in his own world. I
shouldn't complain, there are worse.

RAIN: At least he doesn't beat you.

MAGGIE: I wish he'd at least try to rape me once in awhile.

(*Pause.* RAIN *is caught off-guard.*)

I'm kidding. That was a terrible thing to say.

RAIN: Ash never mentioned your sense of humor—

MAGGIE: Oh I'm just out of practice. What'd you think I was, a dried up old lemon?

RAIN: No, it's a bit unexpected . . . but I like it.

MAGGIE: I hide it from my daughter. She has a very prim and proper image of me and I don't like to disturb that. It'll be our secret. Don't mention the nightgown either. Do we have a deal?

WELFAREWELL

by Cat Delaney

CHARACTERS: ESMERELDA, eighty; ALFRED, her lawyer, middle-aged

CIRCUMSTANCE: Esmerelda Quipp is still of sound mind. Having spent her working life as an actress, she finds that her government pension can't support her. A stint in a women's prison convinces her that jail is the best place to spend her remaining years, and she resorts to a life of crime to get returned to prison.

(ALFRED *and* ESMERELDA *walk downstage to two chairs; the cell upstage goes black.*)

ALFRED: Okay, Mrs. Quipp. Just you and me here. You, me, and the unguarded truth.

ESMERELDA: Protected by the lawyer/client privilege?

ALFRED: Your secret's safe with me.

ESMERELDA: "Foul whisperings are abroad. Unnatural deeds do breed unnatural troubles; infected minds to their deaf pillows will discharge their secrets." It's a simple matter of mathematics, Mr. David. I get a set amount from the government in the form of a pension. It is not sufficient to cover my basic cost of living.

ALFRED: The pundits will say you gave up.

ESMERELDA: My career is over. I aced an audition for the role of Hecate; they gave the part to someone twenty-five years of age. Amateur.

ALFRED: I guess because you're on a pension, you don't qualify for welfare?

ESMERELDA: I have left no stone unturned.

(ALFRED *responds instantly to his ringing cellular telephone.* ESMERELDA *is indignant.*)

ALFRED: Whatsup? . . . Tell him I'll be there within the hour. Bye.

ESMERELDA: Who was that?

(ALFRED *hangs up.*)

ALFRED: My secretary.

ESMERELDA: You were terribly short with her; ring her back and apologize. Go on . . . There's a good lad.

ALFRED: I'm a couple of hours behind here.

ESMERELDA: That's simply no excuse. Ring her.

ALFRED: Look, Mrs. Quipp . . .

ESMERELDA: I'll speak not another word until you behave like the gentleman that your calling suggests. Go on.

(ALFRED *dials his cellular telephone.*)

ALFRED: Yeah, Wendy? Sorry 'bout that. I'm, um, stressed . . .

(ESMERELDA *nods her encouragement.*)

You didn't deserve that . . .

ESMERELDA: (*Whispering.*) Brusque treatment.

ALFRED: Brusque treatment.

ESMERELDA: Excellent good. And . . .

ALFRED: And . . . I owe you lunch . . . Okay, thanks.

(ALFRED *hangs up.*)

ESMERELDA: Is she a nice young lady, your secretary, Wendy?

ALFRED: I guess.

ESMERELDA: Lunch is an excellent good start and you can see how it goes from there.

(ALFRED*'s cellular telephone rings again.*)

ESMERELDA: Kindly do not answer that.

ALFRED: Excuse me?

ESMERELDA: It's frightfully rude. We are speaking about my situation. I require your undivided attention, if you please. I may be destitute now, but I did pay taxes in my day, and those have served, albeit indirectly, to deliver your wages.

ALFRED: Are you being treated for anything, oh, say, medical?

ESMERELDA: Diabetes. Arthritis. Glaucoma. Grief. Old age.

ALFRED: Dementia?

ESMERELDA: "Out, alas! You'd be so lean that blasts of January would blow you through and through.—Now, my fairest friend, I would I had some flowers o' the spring that become your time of day; and yours and yours, that wear upon your virgin branches yet . . . Your maidenheads growing. —O Proserpina, for the flowers now, that, frighted, thou lett'st fall."

ALFRED: I studied Shakespeare at university.

ESMERELDA: Then identify the passage.

ALFRED: *Romeo and Juliet.*

ESMERELDA: That's what they all say.

> "From Dis's wagon! —daffodils, that come before the swallow dares, and take the winds of March with beauty; violets dim, but sweeter than the lids of Juno's eyes or Cytherea's breath; pale primroses . . ."

Can you cite that many lines from a play you don't know the name of?

ALFRED: *The Taming of the Shrew?*

ESMERELDA: *The Winter's Tale.* Dementia? I think not.

ALFRED: Okay, I can probably get you off. There are three possible defenses. Mitigating circumstances. That's one. Your age and general health. That might do it. Or, based on the video, and your waving to the camera, insanity.

ESMERELDA: You look tired. Would you like me to get Jennifer to make you a nice cup of tea? She's got the knack now that an old English lady has taught her properly.

ALFRED: Tea won't cure me, but thanks. What's this about an illegal burial?

ESMERELDA: Ensure the water is at a rolling boil and . . .

ALFRED: I must have the wrong file folder.

ESMERELDA: Never use teabags; a tea ball is crucial.

ALFRED: If you babble on like that in front of a judge . . .

ESMERELDA: I am not insane. The one thing that is working quite well is my mind. Unfortunately.

ALFRED: Unfortunately?

ESMERELDA: Because it leaves me with an acuity that means I know the rest of me is coming unglued. I sometimes think dementia is bliss. One of my old costars is in a nursing home. Hasn't the foggiest what his name is—thinks he's

Oberon—and gets lost going to the closet for his socks, if he remembers why he went to the closet in the first place, but he's full of fun and happily he keeps meeting new people.

ALFRED: How far behind on your payments are you?

ESMERELDA: My prescriptions are paid to current because the chemist does not extend credit. Everything else is far overdue.

ALFRED: When was the last time you ate?

ESMERELDA: I had a rather dry chicken salad sandwich at lunch. I could live off my body fat for a day or two, but the trouble is, I don't have my pills or insulin with me. They took my handbag and all my medications are in it. And my knitting.

ALFRED: I'll take care of that right away. Are you depressed, Mrs. Quipp?

ESMERELDA: Don't be ridiculous! I'm English!

ALFRED: The system provides counseling . . .

ESMERELDA: I require a substantial influx of cash, not a psychiatrist!

ALFRED: You know, I wish I was independently wealthy.

ESMERELDA: That's very kind. Now, go home and get some rest.

ALFRED: I have work to do. You go up in front of the judge tomorrow morning.

ESMERELDA: Not to worry, then. I shall be pleading guilty and throwing myself upon the mercy of the court to give me a nice, long sentence. Officer Hackett tells me that the women's prison has recently been renovated. How charming!

ALFRED: Prisons aren't charming, Mrs. Quipp.

ESMERELDA: Everything is relative, Mr. David.

"Why have you suffer'd me to be imprison'd, kept in a dark house, visited by the priest, and made the most notorious geck and gull that e're invention played on? Tell me why."

LEN AND LOTTIE SCENE FROM

YOU HAVEN'T CHANGED A BIT

by Donna Hoke

CHARACTERS: LOTTIE, seventy, LEN, seventy

CIRCUMSTANCE: Lottie has never been to a high school reunion; Len has been to them all.

LOTTIE: I've missed a lot, haven't I?

LEN: Oh you know how they go.

LOTTIE: Not really. Tell me.

LEN: Well, at the first one, ten years . . . it was a lot of remember this and remember that. And catch-up. Do you have kids? What kind of work do you do? Who's made it and who didn't dare show up. Who got fat. Ten years later, we were all fat. And we counted divorces and remarriages until Carmine started talking about the big game, like he always did, and there was a slide show, and we just ended up remembering a lot more of this and that. I think the next one is when we started talking about how old we were all getting, and thinking it might not be so bad to be back in high school. Then we started losing people and I don't know . . . after that, I think we were just happy to have each other . . . and memories to share with people who knew us when we didn't walk so slowly, when our lives were full of promise, when we first fell in love . . .

LOTTIE: Benjamin Brack. He had a name for the pictures, didn't he? I don't suppose—

LEN: Ninety-eight. Lou Gehrig's.

LOTTIE: I wish I'd known that. I really wish I'd known that.

LEN: I talked to him quite a few times over the years. If it helps, he remembered you fondly.

LOTTIE: As I remember him. Where did the time go?

LEN: Fluttered by like a butterfly. Beautiful. Fleeting.

LOTTIE: That's very poetic, Len. And sad. Sad for Ben, and Patsy, and Mary. I remember them so young. And it's sad that there's no one who sees me like that, that fresh-faced girl and not this old woman.

LEN: I do.

LOTTIE: But I—

LEN: You liked blue sweaters.

LOTTIE: Yes.

LEN: . . . and I liked you in your blue sweaters.

LOTTIE: Len! You're making an old woman blush.

LEN: And you wore your hair in braids on Fridays.

LOTTIE: It was always getting dirty by then.

LEN: Do you remember when I interviewed you for the school paper? You were protesting that girls should be able to play sports. The war was over, and you said you needed a new cause.

LOTTIE: I said that? How self-important you must have thought me.

LEN: Not at all. I took great pride in sharing your views in the *Trumpeter.*

LOTTIE: The *Trumpeter*? My goodness! I haven't thought about that in years.

LEN: You were busy even then. (LEN *reaches into his pocket and pulls out two clippings.*) My earliest bylines.

LOTTIE: (*Reading them.*) By Leonard Bennett. Len Bennett. Oh! Oh my! You're Lenny Benny!

LEN: Nobody has called me that since the last reunion.

LOTTIE: You sat behind me four years in a row in English class. You always asked me how my weekend was.

LEN: Yes!

LOTTIE: And smelled like Mennen.

LEN: That was my dad's.

LOTTIE: And . . . and you asked me to the senior ball before you knew Benjamin had asked me already.

LEN: Yes.

LOTTIE: I can't believe I didn't recognize you. Lenny Benny.

LEN: It's been a long time.

LOTTIE: But you recognized me.

LEN: You haven't changed a bit.

PLAY SOURCES AND ACKNOWLEDGEMENTS

Grateful acknowledgement is made for permission to reprint excerpts from the following:

A Body of Water by Neena Beber. Copyright © 2002 by Neena Beber. Published by Smith and Kraus. All inquiries should be addressed to Mark Subias, United Talent Agency, 888 Seventh Avenue, Seventh Floor, New York, NY 10106.

Abstract Nude by Gwydion Suilebhan. Copyright © 2013 by Gwydion Suilebhan. Reprinted by permission of Original Works Publishing. Complete script and production licensing available from Original Works Publishing. www.originalworksonline.com. Jason Aaron Goldberg, president.

Adoration of the Old Woman by José Rivera. Copyright © 2010 by Jose Rivera. Published by Broadway Play Publishing. All inquiries should be addressed to Jonathan Lomma, William Morris Endeavor Entertainment, 11 Madison Avenue, New York, NY 10010.

Alabama Bound by Charlotte A. Higgins. Copyright © 2015 by Charlotte A. Higgins. Published by Indie Theater Now. Used by permission of Charlotte A. Higgins. All inquiries should be directed to the author at coachcharlotte@yahoo.com.

An Artful Marriage by Martha Patterson. Copyright © 2012 by Martha Paterson & JAC Publishing. Published by JAC

by permission of Bob Ost. All inquiries should be addressed directly to the author at wildlyproductive@gmail.com.

Class by Charles Evered. Copyright © 2010 by Charles Evered. Published by Broadway Play Publishing. Used by permission of Gurman Agency LLC. All inquiries should be addressed to Gurman Agency LLC, at assistant@gurmanagency.com or (212) 749-4618.

Cleaning House by Marj O'Neill-Butler. Copyright © 2015 by Marj O'Neill-Butler. Published by Blue Moon Plays. Used by permission of Marjorie O'Neill-Butler. All inquiries can be made directly to the author at dramamarj@yahoo.com.

Dead and Breathing by Chisa Hutchinson. Copyright © 2017 by Chisa Hutchinson. All rights reserved. Reprinted by permission of Playscripts, Inc. Please contact www.playscripts.com for all inquiries.

Death and the Maiden by Ariel Dorfman. Excerpt(s) from "Death and the Maiden" by Ariel Dorfman, copyright 1992 by Ariel Dorfman. Used by permission of Viking Books, an imprint of Penguin Publishing Group, a division of Penguin Random House LLC. All rights reserved.

Engagement Rules by Rich Orloff. Copyright © 2017 by Rich Orloff. Reprinted by permission of the author. For permission rights and all other matters related to the play, contact Rich Orloff at orloffplays@gmail.com or www.richorloff.com.

Fast Girls by Diana Amsterdam. Copyright © 1989, 1990 by Diana Amsterdam. Reprinted by permission of Samuel French, Inc. CAUTION: Professionals and amateurs are hereby warned that *Fast Girls*, being fully protected under the copyright laws of the United States of America, the British Commonwealth countries, including Canada, and the other countries of the

inquiries should be directed to Nick Hern Books, 49A Goldhawk Road, London, W12 8QP, UK. Email: rights@nickhernbooks. uk.

Home Front by Greg Owens. Copyright © 2006 by Greg Owens. Published by Broadway Play Publishing. Used by permission of Greg Owens. All inquiries should be addressed directly to the author at thegregowens@gmail.com.

How To Make A Rope Swing by Shawn Fisher. Copyright © 2014 by Shawn Fisher. Reprinted by permission of Original Works Publishing. Complete script and production licensing available from Original Works Publishing. www.originalworksonline.com. Jason Aaron Goldberg, president.

My First Pedicure monologue from *I Don't Think So: Life's Stages* by Katherine Burkman. Copyright © 2010 by Katherine H. Burkman. Published by Next Stage Press. Used by permission of Kathrine Burkman. Licensing rights held by Next Stage Press: www.nextstagepress.net.

The Ironing Life by Mary McCullough. Published by the International Centre for Women Playwrights. Used by permission of Mary McCullough. All inquiries should be addressed directly to the author at memm30@yahoo.com.

Juice by Pat Montley. Copyright © 1996 by Pat Montley. Published by Heinemann. Used by permission of Pat Montley. All inquiries should be addressed directly to the author at pat_montley@msn.com or (410) 252-6074.

The Killer and the Comic by Andy Rooster Bloch. Copyright © 2013 by Andy Rooster Bloch. Reprinted by permission of Original Works Publishing. Complete script and production licensing available from Original Works Publishing. www. originalworksonline.com. Jason Aaron Goldberg, president.

was commissioned by The Ensemble Studio Theatre/Alfred P. Sloan Foundation Science & Technology Project and received its world premiere at The Ensemble Studio Theatre on April 8, 2002. *Secret Order* was produced Off-Broadway by Merrimac Repertory Theatre, Charles Towers, Artistic Director; Tom Parrish, Executive Director. Used by permission of Bob Clyman. All inquiries should be addressed to Bret Adams Agency: bretadamsltd.net.

The Secret Wisdom of Trees by Christine Toy Johnson. Copyright © 2015 by Christine Toy Johnson. Published by Indie Theater Now. Used by permission of Christine Toy Johnson. Any inquiries should be addressed directly to the author at www.ChristineToyJohnson.com.

Southern Fried Funeral by J. Dietz Osborne & Nathan Eppler. Copyright © 2015 by J. Dietz Osborne & Nathan Eppler. All rights reserved. Reprinted by permission of Playscript, Inc. Please contact www.playscripts.com for all inquiries.

Spook by Alan Bowne. Copyright © 2015 by Alan Bowne. Published by Broadway Play Publishing. All inquiries should be addressed to Jonathan Lomma, William Morris Endeavor Entertainment, 11 Madison Avenue, New York, NY 10010.

Welfarewell by Cat Delaney. Copyright © 2010 by Cat Delaney. Reprinted by permission of Samuel French, Inc. CAUTION: Professionals and amateurs are hereby warned that *Welfarewell*, being fully protected under the copyright laws of the United States of America, the British Commonwealth countries, including Canada, and the other countries of the Copyright Union, is subject to a royalty. All rights, including professional, amateur, motion picture, recitation, public reading, radio, television, and cable broadcasting, and the rights of

Monologue and Scene Books

Best Contemporary Monologues for Kids Ages 7-15
edited by Lawrence Harbison
9781495011771 ....$16.99

Best Contemporary Monologues for Men 18-35
edited by Lawrence Harbison
9781480369610 ....$16.99

Best Contemporary Monologues for Women 18-35
edited by Lawrence Harbison
9781480369627 ....$16.99

Best Monologues from The Best American Short Plays, Volume Three
edited by William W. Demastes
9781480397408 ....$19.99

Best Monologues from The Best American Short Plays, Volume Two
edited by William W. Demastes
9781480385481 ....$19.99

Best Monologues from The Best American Short Plays, Volume One
edited by William W. Demastes
9781480331556 ....$19.99

Prices, contents, and availability subject to change without notice.

The Best Scenes for Kids Ages 7-15
edited by Lawrence Harbison
9781495011795 ....$16.99

Break the Rules and Get the Part
Thirty Monologues for Women
by Lira Kellerman
9781495075414..........................$12.99

Childsplay
A Collection of Scenes and Monologues for Children
edited by Kerry Muir
9780879101886 ....$16.99

Contemporary Monologues for Twentysomethings
edited by Jessica Bashline
9781495064852..........................$16.99

Contemporary Scenes for Twentysomethings
edited by Jessica Bashline
9781495065446..........................$16.99

Duo!: The Best Scenes for Mature Actors
edited by Stephen Fife
9781480360204 ....$19.99

Duo!: The Best Scenes for Two for the 21st Century
edited by Joyce E. Henry, Rebecca Dunn Jaroff, and Bob Shuman
9781557837028 ....$19.99

Duo!: Best Scenes for the 90's
edited by John Horvath, Lavonne Mueller, and Jack Temchin
9781557830302 ....$18.99

In Performance: Contemporary Monologues for Teens
by JV Mercanti
9781480396616 ....$16.99

In Performance: Contemporary Monologues for Men and Women Late Teens to Twenties
by JV Mercanti
9781480331570 ....$18.99

In Performance: Contemporary Monologues for Men and Women Late Twenties to Thirties
by JV Mercanti
9781480367470 ....$16.99

In Performance: Contemporary Monologues for Men and Women Late Thirties to Forties
by JV Mercanti
9781480396623..........................$16.99

Kids' Comedic Monologues That Are Actually Funny
by Alisha Gaddis
9781495011764..........................$14.99

LGBTQ Comedic Monologues That Are Actually Funny
by Alisha Gaddis
9781495025150..............................$14.99

Later Chapters
The Best Monologues and Scenes for Actors Over Fifty
edited by Diana Amsterdam
9781495072475..............................$16.99

Men's Comedic Monologues That Are Actually Funny
edited by Alisha Gaddis
9781480396814 ....$14.99

One on One: The Best Men's Monologues for the 21st Century
edited by Joyce E. Henry, Rebecca Dunn Jaroff, and Bob Shuman
9781557837011 ....$18.99

Nothing Untoward
Stories from
"The Pumpkin Pie Show"
by Clay McLeod Chapman
9781495061042..............................$19.99

One on One: The Best Women's Monologues for the 21st Century
edited by Joyce E. Henry, Rebecca Dunn Jaroff, and Bob Shuman
9781557837004 ....$18.99

One on One: The Best Men's Monologues for the Nineties
edited by Jack Temchin
9781557831514 ....$12.95

One on One: The Best Women's Monologues for the Nineties
edited by Jack Temchin
9781557831521 ....$11.95

**One on One:
Playing with a Purpose**
Monologues for Kids Ages 7-15
edited by Stephen Fife and Bob Shuman with contributing editors Eloise Rollins-Fife and Marit Shuman
9781557838414 ....$16.99

One on One: The Best Monologues for Mature Actors
edited by Stephen Fife
9781480360198 ....$19.99

Scenes and Monologues of Spiritual Experience from the Best Contemporary Plays
edited by Roger Ellis
9781480331563 ....$19.99

Scenes and Monologues from Steinberg/ATCA New Play Award Finalists, 2008-2012
edited by Bruce Burgun
9781476868783 ....$19.99

Soliloquy!
The Shakespeare Monologues
edited by Michael Earley and Philippa Keil
9780936839783 Men's Edition $12.99
9780936839790 Women's Edition..$14.95

Teen Boys' Comedic Monologues That Are Actually Funny
edited by Alisha Gaddis
9781480396791 ....$14.99

Teen Girls' Comedic Monologues That Are Actually Funny
edited by Alisha Gaddis
9781480396807 ....$14.99

Women's Comedic Monologues That Are Actually Funny
edited by Alisha Gaddis
9781480360426..............................$14.99

APPLAUSE
THEATRE & CINEMA BOOKS
AN IMPRINT OF
HAL•LEONARD
www.halleonardbooks.com

More Acting Titles from Applause

The Best Plays from American Theater Festivals, 2015
edited by John Patrick Bray
9781495057748...............$19.99

5-Minute Plays
edited by Lawrence Harbison
9781495069246...............$16.99

5-Minute Plays for Teens
edited by Lawrence Harbison
9781495069253...............$16.99

How I Did It
Establishing a Playwriting Career
edited by Lawrence Harbison
9781480369634...............$24.99

25 10-Minute Plays for Teens
edited by Lawrence Harbison
9781480387768...............$16.99

More 10-Minute Plays for Teens
edited by Lawrence Harbison
9781495011801...................$9.99

10-Minute Plays for Kids
edited by Lawrence Harbison
9781495053399...................$9.99

The Monologue Audition
A Practical Guide for Actors
by Karen Kohlhaas
9780879102913...............$22.99

The Scene Study Book
Roadmap to Success
by Bruce Miller
9780879103712...............$16.99

Acting Solo
Roadmap to Success
by Bruce Miller
9780879103750...............$16.99

On Singing Onstage
by David Craig
9781557830432...............$18.99

The Stanislavsky Technique: Russia
by Mel Gordon
9780936839080...............$16.95

Speak with Distinction
by Edith Skinner/Revised with New Material Added by Timothy Monich and Lilene Mansell
9781557830470...............$39.99

Recycling Shakespeare
by Charles Marowitz
9781557830944...............$14.95

Actor's Alchemy
Finding the Gold in the Script
by Bruce Miller
9780879103835...............$16.99

Stella Adler—The Art of Acting
compiled & edited by Howard Kissel
9781557833730...............$29.99

Acting in Film
by Michael Caine
9781557832771...............$19.99

The Actor and the Text
by Cicely Berry
9781557831385...............$22.99

The Craftsmen of Dionysus
by Jerome Rockwood
9781557831552...............$19.99

A Performer Prepares
by David Craig
9781557833952...............$19.99

Directing the Action
by Charles Marowitz
9781557830722...............$19.99

Acting in Restoration Comedy
by Simon Callow
9781557831194...............$18.99

The Shakespeare Audition
How to Get Over Your Fear, Find the Right Piece, and Have a Great Audition
by Laura Wayth
9781495010804...............$16.99

The Young Actor's Handbook
by Jeremy Kruse
9781495075421...............$12.99

Accents
A Manual for Actors – Revised & Expanded Edition
by Robert Blumenfeld
9780879109677...............$29.99

Acting with the Voice
The Art of Recording Books
by Robert Blumenfeld
9780879103019...............$19.95

Workshopping the New Play
A Guide for Playwrights, Directors, and Dramaturgs
by George Sapio
9781495088223...............$16.99

The Best American Short Plays 2015-2016
edited by William W. Demastes and John Patrick Bray
9781495065408...............$19.99

The Best Plays of 2015
edited by Lawrence Harbison
9781495045813...............$19.99

The Richard Wesley Play Anthology
by Richard Wesley
9781480394995...............$19.99

Prices, contents, and availability subject to change without notice.